EDITORIAL COLLECTIV

Lara Messersmith-Glavin
Paul Messersmith-Glavin
Maia Ramnath
Sara Rahnoma-Galindo
Kristian Williams

COPYEDITORS

Sam Smith
Em Winokur

DESIGN & LAYOUT

Lantz Arroyo

COVER ART & DESIGN

Josh MacPhee

ARTWORK

Justseeds Artists' Cooperative
Curated by Roger Peet

PRINTING

Charles Overbeck at
Eberhardt Press

Published by
The Institute for
Anarchist Studies

Institute for Anarchist Studies
PO Box 90454
Portland, OR 97290

E-Mail:
anarchiststudies@gmail.com

Web:
anarchiststudies.org

Perspectives Twitter:
@iasperspectives

PERSPECTIVES

RY
19

TABLE OF CONTENTS

BOOK REVIEWS

THANKS

Suzanne Shaffer, Josh MacPhee, Roger Peet, Lantz Arroyo, Charles Overbeck, all the Justseeds artists, Em Winokur, Sam Smith, the Institute for Anarchist Studies collective, the indispensable Sara Libby, our comrades at AK Press, and our generous donors.

THE
TIVE ORDER
the PRISONS
e BORDER

INTRODUCTION

THE PERSPECTIVES
EDITORIAL COLLECTIVE

« Art by the Amor y Resistencia Collective
Justseeds.org

THE WORLD IS ON FIRE. It has been, for quite some time. If you've done any organizing, you've felt it—that sense of racing about, extinguishing this flare up or that, spending precious energy and resources surviving the immediate emergency and hoping the future will somehow save itself. If you've watched the news, you've felt it—disbelief combined with the raw hilarity of the media circus; just when it seems things couldn't get worse, or more frightening, or more absurd, they do. If you've ever worked three jobs to keep your family afloat, you've felt it. If you've listened to climate scientists, or survived a hurricane, or watched helplessly as an unseasonable forest fire tore through a landscape you loved, you've felt it—the rising certainty that we have waited too long, that global temperatures are edging toward tipping points from which we will never return. We are burning.

Western culture has been historically preoccupied with apocalypse, from Judeo-Christian threats of the End Times to doomsday cults. Every generation has imagined themselves living at the edge of history. The anticipation and dread permeate aspects of our puritanical, militaristic, consumeristic culture, yet they offer little in the way of seeing beyond times of crisis. In fact, it seems ever clearer that capitalism thrives on crisis—that capitalism *is* crisis. At this point, could we tell the difference between the "the end is near" and "the end is here?"

What if the apocalypse has already arrived, having crept up incrementally while we were waiting for a big announcement? What if this is what it looks like to be in the thick of things, the "interesting times" of the proverbial curse? Why are we not in the streets, then, in our thousands and our millions? Why haven't we taken over our workplaces and neighborhoods and said, Enough! Are we simply resigned, cynical, nihilistic? Overwhelmed and preoccupied with financial survival? Distracted? Do we even think things can ever radically change for the better, much less in time?

When the Perspectives editorial collective conceived of the "Beyond the Crisis" theme—we admit it, we were feeling pretty apocalyptic. When we started receiving contributions, we were caught off guard by what seemed like a discrepancy between what we were imagining in our projected issue and the work that was submitted. But we soon realized that the writers we were hearing from were indeed answering us— they just responded more strongly to certain parts of our call than others. Namely, they weren't speaking to the post-apocalyptic imaginary and its radical ruptures. They weren't caught up in the same sense of immediacy and lost opportunities. They were exploring ways to proactively navigate sustained, long-game solutions. They wanted to talk about how they have been building a more equitable collective capacity to survive and thrive here, now, where we are—and in the future into which we're heading. That's an interesting thing to observe, and perhaps a partial answer to our curiosity about the current perspectives of anarchist thinkers and organizers.

In this issue, people share the hopes and failures that lead us past the present moment, transcending the mad, reactive hopping from hotspot to hotspot, and instead offer lessons in what German autonomous anti-fascists refer to as "commitment and continuity," or long-term paths out of the fire and into something sustainable, something better. Altogether, the existing experiments discussed in this issue raise questions of how to relate to current structures and institutions in an interim or transitional way, while attempting to move toward more radical alternatives. These institutions are untenable on their own for a variety of reasons, and we must have our own alternative practices, relationships, and organizational forms ready to go as we move forward.

Essays in this issue touch on subjects such as linking children's playthings to utopianism as a way of envisioning a worthwhile future; critically engaging with the traditions of mutual aid, worker co-ops, and municipal governance as ways to counteract the depredations of neoliberal austerity as we advance the socialist project; offering models of self-empowered community-based health alternatives; reflections on an environmental campaign in Ireland exploring lessons about long-term strategy, maintaining sustainable activist communities, and proactive envisioning; and a discussion of several decades of street-level anti-fascist organizing in Germany, which teaches us how to stay self-critical and engaged. These essays and others, plus book reviews related to strategy and organizing, beautiful art by the Justseeds Artists'

Cooperative, and current IAS announcements are what you hold in your hands. We are grateful to Roger Peet for curating the art, Josh MacPhee for his striking cover design, Lantz Arroyo of Radix Media for layout, and Charles Overbeck at Eberhardt Press for printing. We hope that this issue will offer useful reminders of the long-term continuity of our collective projects—yours and ours. We need to carry the fire together, not be consumed by it.

We don't yet know what strategies are going to work, or what life forms and social forms will survive the transition from past to future. We don't know what culture and society will look like—which ingredients it might revitalize from ancestral knowledge systems, and which innovations it might incorporate from emergent social contexts and experiences. There will be transformation. There will be evolution—and revolution. There will continue to be change. It's possible the current political crisis epitomized by Trump will be resolved in a system self-correcting manner, with things going back to "normal," though it's also possible that the present turbulence will result in something qualitatively different. But even if the ruling class resolves the current political crisis in a system-affirming way, that very system is responsible for the ecological crisis, made most obvious in dire climate disruptions, which cannot be solved in the context of capitalism. The civilization that brought us to this point of peril will not be the one that gets us through and out the other side to a society that is ecologically sustainable, equitable, and free. This society must radically change its social, political, and economic structures if humanity is to survive, much less thrive. If there is a new stabilization, it may not look like anything we've known before. So that's an opportunity, a precious chance to implement alternatives long envisioned. Our enemies—whether disaster capitalists, xenophobic nationalistic demagogues, or technotopian accelerationists—never let a good crisis go to waste. Why should we?

CONNECTING OUR STRUGGLES:
BORDER POLITICS, ANTIFASCISM, AND LESSONS FROM THE TRIALS OF FERRERO, SALLITTO, AND GRAHAM

HILLARY LAZAR

« Art by Esther Forbyn | Justseeds.org

I N JANUARY 1940, MARCUS GRAHAM, editor of *Man!: A Journal of the Anarchist Ideal and Movement*, triumphantly declared in a note to the readers that, despite six years of routine government harassment and political persecution, "our journal has endured…our modest voice of truth…[has] carried on." Graham had spoken too soon, as only three additional issues of *Man!* were to appear. After a seven-year run, the periodical folded under the weight of repression and habitual debt. Even so, throughout its duration *Man!* served as a vital voice for the "International Group," an organization with chapters throughout the United States and with ties to several other countries, making it a central connector for a transnational anarchist network involved with antifascist resistance.

Now, close to eighty years later, one of the lesser known moments in anarchist history, the efforts to suppress *Man!*—including the several-year legal persecution and deportation trials of the editor, Marcus Graham, and his associates Vincenzo Ferrero and Domenic Sallitto—provide an important window into mechanisms of state control by serving as a powerful example of the connections between border politics, immigration policy, and political repression. As their cases show, deportation and the active exclusion or removal of certain populations are among the governmental tools used to quell dissent. Moreover, reactionary nativist fears are easily leveraged—particularly during periods of national crisis or instability—and help to further fuel intensified targeting of immigrants, radicals, and other marginalized people perceived as threatening to the status quo. In essence, then, what we see in these trials is that it is impossible to decouple the racialized, colonial project of determining who qualifies as a desirable or legitimate citizen from efforts to suppress political opposition. Furthermore, it is a stark reminder that what is happening in today's political climate around immigration policy and the criminalization of dissent, while certainly egregious, is part of a much longer historical pattern.

MAN!, THE INTERNATIONAL GROUP, AND THE TRIALS OF FERRERO, SALLITTO, AND GRAHAM

Man! first appeared in January 1933 after Vincenzo Ferrero, former editor of the Italian-American anarchist periodical L'Emancipazione, recruited Romanian-born Marcus Graham (née Shmuel Marcus) to help establish it as an English-language version of and successor to the earlier paper. In effect, it was intended to promote the more militant, individualist, and insurrectionary form of Galleanist anarchism—named for Italian-American anarchist, Luigi Galleani (1861–1931), known for his advocacy of "propaganda by the deed" and militant opposition to the state—evident in the contributors' frequent derisions of more organized forms of resistance such as federative models and syndicalism. As the paper promised in its first issue, *Man!* offered "no programs, platforms or palliatives on any of the social issues confronting mankind;" rather, it was for "those who are willing to face the truth, and act for themselves" and enable "[m]an to regain confidence in himself, in his great power to achieve liberation from every form of slavery that now encircles him." The journal was also an important voice for antifascism and was vehemently anti-racist—often including pieces related to racial inequality in its running commentary on local, national, and international news—along with paying attention to labor issues, instances of political repression, and antifascist efforts in Europe. And under Graham's editorship, it took on a proto-green, primitivist tone in its anti-technology stance as well.

Although *Man!* was initially only available in California, within two years of its appearance, it boasted readership in "every state in the union." Eventually its circulation extended to locations as far spread as Cuba, the UK, Germany, Japan, New Zealand, Australia, and Palestine. Published in San Francisco, it eventually came to be the group's main organ and the heart of very active anarchist communities, which (much akin to anarchist groups today) hosted frequent gatherings such as spaghetti dinners and picnics as fundraisers for political prisoners; radical art, music, and theater performances; and, of course, speaker events and panels, including talks on the rise of fascism and report-backs on anarchist efforts in the Spanish Civil War. Co-founded by Ferrero in 1927, the International Group was meant to be a way to bring together the numerous multi-ethnic anarchist communities in the Bay Area—including Chinese,

Mexican, French, Russian, and Italian groups—and was, in part, modeled after the International Group of New York, which had been established to help support publication of the New York–based anarchist paper *Road to Freedom* (with which Graham had been involved). Again, reflecting the Galleanist anti-organizational stance, it rejected a federative model and favored a looser coalition that provided events and activities, like the publication of *Man!*, that allowed them to come together more informally. And in fact, within months of the periodical's launch on New Year's Eve 1932, it reported that unofficial chapters and friends of the International Group around the country in cities like New York, Chicago, Detroit, Patterson, and Philadelphia were helping to support its publication.

Little more than a year following its debut, however, the local and federal government began to systematically harass the paper's subscribers. In the May 1934 issue, Graham reports that readers were sending letters of complaint regarding visits from government agents. The officials had been detaining them at the local justice departments for questioning on their relationship with the periodical, demanding to know "why they read and lent material aid to an Anarchist journal such as *Man!*." Sessions ended with threats of deportation against the foreign-born readers and criminal prosecution for those born in America. Meanwhile, a hold had been placed on the journal, preventing the March issue from reaching many of its readers. Despite these attempts to intimidate *Man!*'s followers and the members of the International Group, their commitment did not waiver. Letters continued to pour in, the gatherings went on, and every month individuals and organizations scraped together money to ensure that the next issue would appear. Yet, the government's harassment of *Man!*'s readers and the delays in its distribution were just the beginning.

> "THE GOVERNMENT'S HARASSMENT OF MAN'S READERS AND THE DELAYS IN ITS DISTRIBUTION WERE JUST THE BEGINNING."

On April 11, 1934, immigration inspectors and local police led by E. C. Benson forcibly entered the restaurant owned and operated by Vincenzo Ferrero and Domenic Sallitto in Oakland, California, and raided the small space at the back of their business rented to Graham for use as the printing headquarters for *Man!*. Although Ferrero had been the one to initially suggest that Graham start the paper, neither he nor Sallitto officially contributed to its publication. Both, however, were well known for their ties to the Italian-American anarchist communities in San Francisco and New York, and for their vocal opposition to Mussolini. Consequently, after the inspectors ransacked the backroom to obtain copies of the periodical and materials used for its production, they were both arrested on "telegraphic warrants from Washington to be seized for deportation." Ferrero was then charged with "causing the publication of *Man!*," and Sallitto was picked up for chairing a debate on Dutch antifascist Marinus van der Lubbe the previous March, during which he purportedly advocated the violent overthrow of the government. Each was quickly released on a thousand-dollar bond apiece, secured with help from Rose Pesotta, a New York anarchist who had risen to the position of vice president for the International Ladies' Garment Workers' Union.

Only nine days later, however, a squad of detectives returned, allegedly in response to an attempted robbery of the restaurant, and raided the office for a second time. The two men were removed to Angel Island, off the coast of San Francisco—the West Coast version of Ellis Island, where immigrants were often detained prior to deportation proceedings—and it became clear that their charges were not readily going to be dropped.

For a year, the cases of Ferrero and Sallitto remained at a standstill as they went in and out of custody, all the while working tirelessly with advocates from the International Group in concert with legal counsel from the American Committee for Protection of Foreign Born (ACPFB), an affiliate of the American Civil Liberties Union (ACLU).

"IMMIGRATION POLICY AND DEPORTATION ARE EXPLICITLY TIED TO ANTI-RADICAL EFFORTS BECAUSE THEY SERVE AS ONE OF THE PRIMARY TOOLS USED IN POLITICAL SUPPRESSION."

Then in June 1935, when their verdict did finally come in, they were dealt a crushing blow. Even though they were both legal residents of the United States—Ferrero, a thirty-year resident, and Sallitto, a fifteen-year resident and widowed father of a three-year-old daughter born to an American wife—the Bureau of Immigration of the Labor Department ordered their deportation to Italy. On December 10, 1935, the United States' Labor department issued a formal demand that Ferrero turn himself in to Ellis Island for the sailing of the SS *Conte di Savoia* to Italy two weeks later. He complied and arrived a day prior to his scheduled departure date. His attorney, however, managed to stay the deportation through a writ of habeas corpus. Sallitto joined his comrade at Ellis Island shortly thereafter, as he was scheduled to be deported on January eleventh. Like Ferrero, he also secured a writ of habeas corpus, and after three months of detention, both men were released. Nevertheless, their legal persecution was not over.

Ultimately charged with "being a member of an organization advocating the overthrow of government by force and violence," Sallitto's ordeal persisted for two additional years. It was not until January 1938, following four years of legal proceedings and several months of detention at both Ellis and Angel Islands—which meant prolonged periods of separation from his young daughter of whom he had sole custody—that his case was dismissed. Ferrero did not fare so well. While the court never directly determined that he was involved with *Man!* in any official capacity, as the former editor of the Italian anarchist periodical *L'Emancipazione*, he was charged with "writing or publishing printed material advocating the overthrow of government by force and violence." And despite his claims that he qualified for political asylum because being sent back to Italy would condemn him to severe punishment for having "written and spoke violently against Mussolini for years," in February 1937, the Second District Court of Appeals denied his plea. Ferrero, meanwhile, was still slated for deportation in November 1939, but he managed to jump bail and then went off the radar by assuming the alias "Johnny the Cook" back in California.

Throughout the years of Ferrero and Sallitto's persecution, Graham faced similar tribulations. A few days prior to June 11, 1936, he received a notice from the

Bureau of Immigration upholding a mandate for his deportation issued seventeen years earlier. The nearly two-decade-old directive demanded his return to Canada, where he allegedly held citizenship, for the crime of possessing subversive anarchist literature. Graham was denied entry into Canada, and the immigration officials, unable to ascertain his nation of origin, allowed the expulsion to slip through the legal cracks. With pressure on the rise to shut down *Man!*, Graham felt threatened enough by the renewed interested in his expulsion to go underground. And in the August–September 1936 issue, he announced his termination as editor of *Man!*. He then temporarily entrusted its editorship to Ray Randall and Walter Brooks (pseudonyms for Sallitto and his partner Aurora Alleva, a prominent second-generation anarchist and antifascist from Philadelphia), although under Hippolyte Havel's name, and for a year the periodical was published out of New York. The following July, Graham came out of hiding and reassumed his role as editor, relocating its headquarters to Los Angeles.

Graham's return was short lived. It was only two months before the authorities once again took action against him. On October 6, 1937, four plainclothes immigration officers raided the Los Angeles office and seized all materials relating to *Man!*. Graham was arrested on site and incarcerated in the county jail for eight days. Several months of hearings and appeals followed, and on January 14, 1938, Judge Leon R. Yankovich finally dismissed the seventeen-year-old edict. Nonetheless, Graham did not evade all legal repercussions. Judge Yankovich sentenced him to six months imprisonment on the charge of "criminal contempt" for his persistent refusal to reveal his place of birth to immigration officials, which made it impossible deport him. Again, he managed to temporarily elude his punishment with additional legal appeals, although it was a Pyrrhic victory. By this point, sufficient damage had been done to the stability of *Man!*'s publication that it was now deeply in debt. With the aid of contributions from supporters, *Man!* stayed afloat for another year and a half, but in April 1940, the US district attorney "advised" the journal's printer to immediately suspend the printing of the May issue. When Graham was unable to find an alternate publisher, he was forced to end its run. Two months later he lost his appeal regarding the pending charge of contempt for refusing to cooperate with immigration officials, and was sentenced to serve out his time.

THE BIGGER PICTURE: IMMIGRATION POLICY AND DEPORTATION AS STATE CONTROL AND POLITICAL REPRESSION

There are critical lessons to be found in the ways these trials and the targeting of *Man!* elucidate border politics and the racialized, ideological aspects of citizenship and state control. To begin with, this story points not only to a long history of anti-anarchist and anti-immigrant sentiments in the United States (no real shocker here), but more specifically to the connections between them. Immigration policy and deportation are explicitly tied to anti-radical efforts because they serve as one of the primary tools used in political suppression. Furthermore, to make this link is also to underscore how these structures must be understood as reflective of the larger white supremacist, imperial projects of state making, through their determination of who can stay, who goes, and what political views they can hold.

Adelante, companeros!

Throughout America's early history, laws such as the Alien and Sedition Acts of 1798 and the Indian Removal Act of 1830 were aimed at the elimination of unwanted groups. Signed into law by President John Adams, the former made naturalization more difficult and allowed for imprisonment and deportation of "dangerous" foreign-born residents or of those critical of the government, while the latter was intended to help clear land for white settlers. It was with the Supreme Court ruling in *Fong Yue Ting v. United States* in 1893, however, that all constitutional safeguards against the expulsion of immigrants were eliminated, opening the floodgates to the use of deportation as a tool of political repression and social control. It was in this case that deportation was determined to be an "administrative" process rather than a criminal matter—and hence, not subject to due process.

Following this ruling, immigrants were subject to expulsion based on star-chamber examinations and the arbitrary finding that they were somehow "inconsistent with public welfare." There was also no longer a legal bar against lengthy incarcerations, repeated searches and seizures of their property, high bail, and self-incrimination. Furthermore, the process was now, above all, to be based on expedience. This allowed for practices such as use of the telegraphic warrants, which effectively enabled immigration officers to round up noncitizens on a basis of "guilty until proven innocent." It was this ruling, in hand with the "Anarchist Act" of 1903 as well as the hyper-patriotic Espionage and Sedition Acts of 1917 and 1918—which made anarchists inadmissible for US entry and enabled denaturalization and deportation of any foreign-born resident who opposed the government—that effectively shaped federal policy for nonresident radicals during the first decades of the twentieth century. Together, these paved the way for roundups like the Palmer Raids in 1919 (resulting in the detention of 10,000 suspected radicals, 1,000 of whom were deported to Russia), and two decades later the detention of Ferrero, Sallitto, and Graham.

Immigration policy was also used to curtail potential "foreign threats" by proactively preventing entry of certain ethnic groups or immigrants with suspect political beliefs to the United States. In the decade just preceding the Depression, for example, amid the post–World War I anti-immigrant hysteria and rise of white supremacist nativism, the Immigration Acts of 1921 and 1924, including the National Origins Act of 1924—designed to impede further immigration by Southern and Eastern Europeans and exclude Asians and Africans—instituted a 2 percent cap per country based on their total population in the 1890 census. Then, during World War II (notably, overlapping time wise with Graham's trial and occurring shortly after the final verdicts came in for Ferrero and Sallitto), the government passed a barrage of anti-immigrant bills including the Foreign Agents Registration Act of 1938, requiring all agents for foreign principles to register with the Secretary of State. A few years later, following the war and as anti-Communist Cold War hysteria set in, the United States passed the McCarran-Walter Act, which again seriously capped entry of Asians while establishing ideological criteria for expulsion—any immigrant or foreign-born resident could be expelled for "activities prejudicial to the public interest" or "subversive to national security."

The political and economic instability of the Great Depression only added to the intensity of the xenophobic and anti-radical sentiment driving the efforts to deport Graham, Ferrero, and Sallitto. Tensions ran particularly high in California, where there was a deep history of conservative nativism and vigilantism. It was California, for instance, that served as the heart of the anti-Chinese movement in the late nineteenth century, which eventually led to the Chinese Exclusion Act of 1882. Then in 1916, anxieties over labor agitation allowed fear to trump justice when radical labor activist Tom Mooney and his assistant, Warren K. Billings, were incarcerated for twenty-three years, despite their obvious innocence, for the bombing of the San Francisco Preparedness Day parade. And of thirty-three states to pass criminal syndicalism acts in the wake of the Palmer Raids, California was one of the only ones to actually keep the law on the books, rounding up some 504 members of the Industrial Workers of the World (IWW) before it was repealed in 1924.

By the 1930s, California not only served as home to one of the most extensive and well-organized radical networks in the United Sates but also had an economy that depended on immigrant labor. With agribusiness the dominant industry, Mexican migrant workers were in many ways the backbone of the state's financial well-being. Asian Americans were also a major source of labor for the farms. For this reason, the intersection of the radical presence with the large, agricultural workforce, gave rise to a powerful immigrant-based farm workers' movement. This growth in organized labor, coupled with the established pattern of scapegoating noncitizens and radicals during economic panics, and with California's propensity for vigilantism, elicited an aggressive nativist and anti-radical response from the local elite: hundreds of thousands of Mexicans were coerced or convinced into repatriating during the 1930s; and, while not all faced deportation, many Southern and Eastern European radicals experienced political persecution and xenophobic harassment along the lines of that endured by the members of the International Group.

It was the longshoremen and maritime worker's General Strike of July 1934, though, that served as the immediate backdrop for the suppression of *Man!*. In May 1934, longshoremen had shut down every port along the West Coast, sparking bloody battles and rioting in several of the major cities, including San Francisco. This came to a head following the killing of a striker and sympathizer during a clash with local police, which led to a citywide General Strike. Although it lasted only four days, the National Guard, local authorities, and vigilantes responded with a heavy counteroffensive that targeted ethnic radical groups and, in particular, anarchists and communists. It comes as no surprise that only a month before the initial coast-wide walkout by the longshoremen, local officials began rounding up suspected radical immigrants and tightening the reins on the distribution of pro-labor printed materials like *Man!* The successful suppression of *Man!* and the vigorous efforts to deport these men represented both a desperate attempt to deter further labor agitation and demonstrate the government and local authorities' abilities to reassert their control during a period of upheaval. As anarchist historian Kenyon Zimmer points out, its supression also reflects the racial dimensions of their political persecution. Critiques of anarchist agitators, he observes, were impossible to disentangle from xenophobic sentiment and the popular perception that their radicalism was due to ethnic and/or biological deficiencies. Effectively, foreign-born radicals, particularly those from Southern and Eastern Europe who were denied full access to "whiteness," were racialized because of their political beliefs.

IMMIGRATION POLICY AND THE CRIMINALIZATION OF DISSENT TODAY

Much of what we see in the story of these trials and the efforts to suppress *Man!* is mirrored in what is happening today under Trump, both in terms of the leveraging of immigration policy and use of deportation as a way to advance a white supremacist, imperial agenda, and in the ways this is tied to the criminalization of dissent. Indeed, there are even direct parallels in terms of the procedural mechanisms and policies being put into place now that were explicitly used in the 1930s to attack immigrant communities and activist voices, including antifascist resistors such as those involved with *Man!*.

After coming to power, one of Trump's first acts was to call for the anti-Muslim travel ban, which like earlier policies barred entry based on racial/ethnic status and country of origin. In this case, the ban targeted anyone from an Islamic-majority country (save from US-friendly Saudi Arabia), and it was justified using the post-9/11 language of anti-terrorism. While ultimately this effort failed—in no small part due to pressure put on the federal courts by the widespread "airport protests" that erupted in response to the measure—Trump and his supporters continue to advocate for this kind of ban. In fact, Jeff Sessions is on record as praising the 1924 Johnson-Reed Act, which included the National Origins Act (the policy that banned immigrants from Asia entirely and severely curtailed Eastern and Southern European migration, with a specific intent to target Italians, Jews, Africans, and Middle Easterners), as a model to be followed by the Trump administration.

Trump also signed off on changes to a program known as 287(g) within the Department of Homeland Security (DHS) that implemented draconian new policies, which included expedited deportation processes, increased mass detentions, and use of local police and deputies as de facto immigration agents, allowing them to arrest and detain any person who *may* be in violation of immigration laws. Nearly forty law enforcement agencies participate in this program and, according to the Immigrant Legal Resource Center, nearly all were already unofficially working in collaboration prior to the formalized arrangement. Following its enactment between January and September of 2017, there was 42 percent increase in detention of immigrants living within the United States. Meanwhile, arrests of immigrants with no criminal convictions nearly tripled. It is likely that in 2018, the attack on immigrants will only further intensify, as Immigration and Customs Enforcement (ICE) intends to significantly augment the daily population of detainees.

Certainly, this is not to suggest that contemporary efforts to control dissent through determination of who constitutes a "good" citizen are unique to the Trump administration. Despite the liberal misperception that the United States has largely been welcoming to immigrants since it banned caps based on country of origin in the 1965 Immigration and Naturalization Act, it has in fact continued to enact procedures that severely curtail the rights and liberties of residents based on country of origin and legal status, and that operate in ways incongruous with due process. In the wake of 9/11, for instance, it was the Bush administration that first created the 273(g) program and established DHS and ICE. Bush also passed a law allowing for "stipulated removal," which as of 2011 had enabled the deportation of more than 160,000 noncitizens without hearings before immigration judges. Moreover, whether or not immigrant detainees are granted due process was (and continues to be) largely determined by their ability to afford legal counsel. This class-determinative basis for who has access to legal rights was again recently upheld in a hearing that ruled against the constitutionality of requiring free counsel for immigrant children facing deportation who cannot pay for legal fees. As it stands, more than half the immigrants facing deportation hearings are unrepresented. By denying the right to periodic bond hearings, the US Supreme Court has also backed indefinite detention for immigrants, including both those with permanent legal status and asylum seekers. On average, detainees are held for over a year.

In addition, the United States has one of the largest immigration detention infrastructures in the world and detains more than 400,000 annually, including legal permanent residents, asylum seekers, and victims of human trafficking. Contemporary immigrant detention was first established as a standard procedure in the '80s but doubled under Clinton with passage of the Antiterrorism and Effective Death Penalty Act (AEDPA) and the Illegal Immigration Reform and Immigrant Responsibility Act (IIRIRA), and has ballooned in the twenty-first century due to mandatory lockup quotas. More recently, despite Deferred Action for Childhood Arrivals (DACA) and the Development, Relief, and Education for Alien Minors Act (DREAM) Act, Obama was responsible for some of the largest "return" and "removal" practices—deporting over 3 million during his eight years in office. And in 2010, Arizona passed SB 1070, which has served as a model for numerous states, effectively institutionalizing racial profiling and legitimating police demands for paperwork based on appearance or "suspicion" alone.

At the same time, there has been a dangerous trend toward the criminalization of protest. One of the best-publicized instances of this, of course, was the arrest of 234 people—including medics, legal observers, and journalists—for participating in an anti-capitalist, anti-fascist march during the J20 protests against Trump's inauguration. Of them, 194 faced multiple felony charges and up to seventy-five years in prison. Yet, the attacks on dissent include everything from the labeling of environmental protestors "domestic terrorists," to governmental surveillance of racial justice activists, to the local anti-protest laws proposed in eighteen states. Much akin to the mass arrests of the J20 protests, on October 22, 2017, over 800 water protectors were arrested near the Standing Rock Reservation while protesting the Dakota Access Pipeline. Over 300 remain on trial. And there has also been an explicit linkage across these efforts that has developed as law enforcement and immigration officers have specifically targeted those known as activists and community leaders. In fact, a federal lawsuit has been brought against ICE for unconstitutional surveillance in response to the detention of Jean Montrevil and Ravi Ragbir, leaders of the New Sanctuary Coalition of New York City. Montrevil was deported to Haiti, while Ragbir's deportation was stayed by a judge because of ongoing legal proceedings. As was the case for Ferrero, Sallitto, and Graham, however, these trials are only part of a larger effort to suppress the group and silence its member through political harassment such as surveillance, raids, and arrests.

Montrevil and Ragbir are not the only examples—there's Maru Mora Villalpando, a Mexican national in Washington state who helped to publicize detainees' hunger strikes; Eliseo Jurado in Boulder, Colorado, who has been public in challenging his wife's deportation to Peru; Martín Esquivel-Hernández, an activist and community leader in Pittsburgh, was detained and deported after participating in an immigrant rights May Day rally; the list goes on.

Furthermore, the deputization of police as ICE agents only deepens the potential for racialized profiling of immigrants (in particular, undocumented and queer or trans folks), who are at disproportionate risk for targeting by law enforcement. Again, this is reflected in the numbers: while only 7 percent of noncitizens in the United States are Black, they make up 20 percent of those facing deportation on criminal grounds. Nor is this tie between the criminalization of race and political protest anything new. The very same Riot Act used in the prosecution of the J20 protestors, for instance, was initially passed as a way to quell anti-racist uprisings in 1967 and used to put down the DC rebellion following the murder of Martin Luther King Jr. in 1968, which resulted in some 6,100 arrests.

LESSONS FOR TODAY...AND A HOPEFUL AFTERWORD?

Ultimately, the story of *Man!*'s suppression and the trials of Ferrero, Sallitto, and Graham serve as another reminder of the long, interwoven history of racist, xenophobic, classist, and anti-radical (and even explicitly anti-anarchist) mechanisms of state control. These include policies that confer or deny legal status to certain populations based on racial or ethnic criteria, political beliefs, or other criteria—along with use of detention, deportation, and denial of due process. And in some cases, there may even be active collusion between civilians and the state through both formal and informal arrangements, such as deputized law enforcement, citizen militias, and other forms of private surveillance. There is also a direct correlation to the carceral state at large—beyond that which applies to immigrants, radicals, and radical immigrants.

While reforms may grant access or "legitimacy" to certain individuals or populations, it will only be through the abolition of the white supremacist imperialism of the nation-state and these interconnected systems of control—from prisons and policing to border imperialism and the national security state—that all peoples will be allowed full status as valued, free individuals in our society. Indeed, as decolonial thinkers like Harsha Walia in *Undoing Border Imperialism* point out, this means adopting a more liberatory approach to immigrant solidarity—one that shifts attention from ensuring citizenship toward challenging capitalism and settler colonialism, and the settler state itself. As is evident in the story of these trials, doing so also necessitates recognition of the inherent ties between border imperialism and control of political dissent. And more importantly, it means understanding that these mechanisms of domination are expressly tied to *all* forms of structural oppression, which are at the root of the state-based logic and domination. In essence, then, what we really need is to dismantle the underpinning, interlocking systems of oppression if we're to see an end to the kind of logic and praxis—including immigration policy and laws tied to the criminalization of protest—that allow for the determination of human value and access to freedom to be based on national origin and on political support for the colonial state.

There is also a welcome message of hope in this story. Despite the rise of fascism in the 1930s and the clear evidence of authoritarian, proto-fascist elements involved in the attack on *Man!* and those associated with it, there is also evidence of a vital transnational solidarity effort that sprang up in response, which not only helped to cement connections across borders, but energized and empowered anti-fascist resistance.

Ironically, if the goal of Graham, Ferrero, and Sallitto's persecution was to deter further radical agitation, it instead helped to unite the American Left in one of the largest protest movements of the period. The ACLU, which immediately took on their cases, made sure to spread word on the issue to the wider public. Over barely more than a year following the initial raid, hundreds of organizations and thousands of individuals joined protests on their behalf throughout the country. The first public gathering was held on July 2, 1935, at the San Francisco Labor College. Spokespeople at the event represented numerous labor and radical organizations including the ACLU; the IWW; the International Group; the International Ladies' Garment Workers Union;

the Non-Partisan Labor Defense; the Proletarian, Workers' and Socialist Parties; and the Tom Mooney Molders' Defense Committee. Soon thereafter, on July 22nd, the Ferrero-Sallitto Defense Conference was established at the Stuyvesant Casino in New York, and six days later the first mass demonstration outside of California was held at Union Square.

Following this demonstration, largely under the coordination of Aurora Alleva (secretary of the Ferrero-Sallitto Defense Conference), along with Rose Pesotta and Italian anarchist Valerio Isca, numerous committees were formed across the country as part of the effort to arrange local demonstrations and inundate Capitol Hill with letters of protest. Another rally held at Irving Plaza in New York City on October 27, 1935, had delegates from some 221 organizations, all of whom signed a declaration "that the traditional right of asylum in America for political and religious refugees from tyrannical governments be preserved." Copies of the resolution were sent directly to President Roosevelt. Within six months, in addition to New York and San Francisco, major protests were also held in Philadelphia, Chicago, Cleveland and Los Angeles. Meanwhile, after Graham's arrest, separate defense committees were formed out of many of the same groups on his behalf.

The movement to see justice for Ferrero, Sallitto, and Graham continued to grow in size and intensity, catching the attention of numerous prominent citizens who joined the defense committees, often taking on coordinating roles for the protests and petitions. Multiple delegations of notable personalities, civil rights advocates, and labor leaders even went so far as to travel to Washington to contest Secretary of Labor Perkins's sign-off on their deportation. On December 23, 1935, five members of the Conference met with Assistant Secretary of Labor Edward McGrady to no avail. When that failed, another attempt to intercede on their behalf was made by "100 renown[ed] men and women in the realm of Art and Education." And by January 1938 upward of 40,000 letters of protest representing 500,000 individuals were sent to Secretary of Labor Frances Perkins. Several high-profile individuals, including Sherwood Anderson, Roger Baldwin, Alice Stone Blackwell, John Dewey, Max Eastman, Kate Crane-Gartz, Sinclair Lewis, Scott Nearing, Jon Dos Passos, Upton Sinclair, and Norman Thomas were among them.

It was not only the United States, however, that saw a surge of solidarity on their behalf. Letters continued to pour in from abroad in support of their legal efforts. And along with the defense chapters established in the United States, there was also defense support in France, Spain, Italy, and Switzerland—notably countries where there were large antifascist, anarchist presences. Indeed, as those involved in the efforts maintained, the fact that Ferrero and Sallitto were prominent anti-fascist organizers, along with the trial of Graham's and the suppression of *Man!*, was indicative of a nascent fascist element in the United States—thus, work on their behalf was further tied to resistance abroad.

Despite the widespread international attention their trials received, however, during which Ferrero was officially slated for deportation and Graham jailed for half a year, the protests had only met with partial success. The International Group simply could not withstand the weight of the persecution. *Man!* folded and the network disbanded. Even so, members of the group itself, along with other comrades who had been involved with the defense, went on to do critical work in the years to come—from helping with new journals such as *Why?*, to radical projects like the Walden School in Berkeley, to serving as mentors for the anti-war activists of the 1960s and beyond. Indeed, the solidarity movement on their behalf had helped to radicalize a new generation of anarchists, some of whom remained active throughout the anti-globalization days. In other words, even in the face of defeat, there were still important strands of hope carried on by the individuals, relationships, and networks that emerged from those trials. And for several years, the trials had served as a formative transnational rallying point across the radical and progressive Left, including among those involved in antifascist resistance.

That said, approaching a century later, we're still seeing the very same mechanisms of control wielded against antifascist, anarchist, and immigrant communities—not to mention against other communities of color and marginalized populations. So, organizers today: take heart in the wins of their story, but also consider it a reminder that our goal should be to learn from histories such as these, and to continue working toward the elimination of the settler, carceral state that determines who is "legitimate" and who is "criminal." Particularly in moments such as the present one—where reactionary, fascist, white supremacist forces are further emboldened by the state and political climate—it is essential to understand that our struggles are connected, in some cases, even in their historical origins.

ABOUT THE AUTHOR

Hillary Lazar is a doctoral candidate in Sociology at the University of Pittsburgh, where she teaches about social movements, gender, power and resistance through an anarchist lens. She is currently researching personal transformation in prefigurative spaces. Hillary has been published in Perspectives on Anarchist Theory, *contributed a chapter to* Anarchism: A Conceptual Approach (2018), *and has worked on several other book projects, including* Emma Goldman: A Documentary History of the American Years (2003). *She is a collective member of the Big Idea Bookstore, a content editor for Agency: An Anarchist PR Project, instructor for the Institute for Advanced Troublemaking, and is involved in graduate student worker organizing.*

Research and writing of this essay was made possible, in part, by a writing grant from the Institute for Anarchist Studies.

ENDNOTES

1   Marcus Graham, "Our Eighth Year," *Man!, A Journal of Anarchist Movement and Ideal,* January 1940 (Connecticut: Greenwood Reprint Corporation, 1970).

2   For two of the best accounts of *Man!* and the International Group, see Kenyon Zimmer, *Immigrants Against the state: Yiddish and Italian Anarchism in America* (Chicago: University of Illinois, 2015), 178–218; and Andrew Cornell, Unruly Equality: US Anarchism in the Twentieth Century (Berkeley: University of California Press, 2016), 114–120. For an excellent and in-depth account of the trials, as well as analysis of the ties between citizenship, race, and political ideology, see Zimmer's chapter "Positively stateless: Marcus Graham, the Ferrero-Sallitto Case, and Anarchist Challenges to Race and Deportation," in Moon-Ho Jung, ed., *The Rising Tide of Color: Race, state Violence, and Radical Movements Across the Pacific* (University of Washington Press, 2014), 128–158. Zimmer argues that not only must we understand these as connected, but specifically that anarchist embracing of "statelessness" was a strategic way to resist state control as it called into question the logic of the nation-state and also actively impeded deportation proceedings. For additional biographical information on Ferrero (aka "Johnny the Cook") and Sallitto, see the brief oral histories by them in Paul Avrich's *Anarchist Voices: An Oral History of Anarchism in America* (Oakland: AK Press, 2005). Graham also provides some additional commentary in his "Autobiographical Note," in the foreword to his anthology, *Man! An Anthology of Anarchist Ideas, Essays, Poetry and Commentaries* (London: Cienfuegos Press, 1974).

3   *Man!,* January 1933. Galleanist anarchism was named after Luigi Galleani (1861–1931), an Italian-American anarchist who founded the anarchist periodical Cronaca Sovversiva, which ran from 1903–1920. Galleani and his supporters (including Sacco and Vanzetti) were known for their promotion of "propaganda by the deed," or direct action and militant opposition to the state. For more on Galleani and Italian-American anarchism, see Travis Tomchuck, *Transnational Radicals: Italian Anarchists in Canada and the US*, 1915–1940 (University of Manitoba, 2015). For detailed accounts of Man's politics, see Cornell, *Unruly Equality*, 114–118 and Zimmer, "Positively stateless."

4   See, for instance, articles in *Man!,* including: "Onward-People of Spain," August–September 1936; "Behind the Lines of Spain," October–November 1936; "They Shall Not Pass," December 1936–Janaury 1937; and "Save Spain Save Yourselves," February–March 1937. See also Cornell, *Unruly Equality*, 100–118.

5   *Cornell, Unruly Equality*, 100–118.

6   "The Movement Around Man," *Man!,* May–June 1933.

7   *Man!,* March 1934.

8   The New York International Group was actually the informal name for the Road to Freedom Group that published Road to Freedom, a journal edited by Hyppolite Havel from 1927–1931, which is considered by many to be the successor to Emma Goldman's periodical *Mother Earth.* Several of the oral histories in Avrich's *Anarchist Voices* (2005) refer to the Road to Freedom Group.

9   See Zimmer, *Immigrants Against the state*, 195; and "Positively stateless," 128–158; see also Cornell, *Unruly Equality*, 100–118.

10   "Government's Foul Conspiracy to Destroy *Man!*," *Man!*, May 1934.

11   Along with Ferrero's account, there is also a brief oral history by Sallitto in Paul Avrich's *Anarchist Voices: An Oral History*, 160–167.

12   "Government's Foul Conspiracy to Destroy *Man!*," *Man!*, May 1934.

13   Cornell, *Unruly Equality*, 115; Zimmer, *Immigrants Against the state*, 180–183.

14   "Government's Foul Conspiracy to Destroy *Man!*," *Man!*, May 1934.

15   "Alleged Anarchist Fights Deportation," *San Francisco Chronicle*, September 5, 1935; "Deportation Order Fought," *San Francisco Chronicle*, December 29, 1935; "Resisting Attempt to Throttle Freedom of Thought," *Man!*, July–August 1935; "Deportations Hysteria," *Man!*, October–November 1936.

16   "The Struggle to Save Ferrero and Sallitto," *Man!*, January 1936; "Deportation Order Fought," *San Francisco Chronicle*, December 29, 1935.

17   "Bay Man Appeals Deportation Order," *San Francisco Chronicle*, October 8, 1936; "The Ferrero and Sallitto Case," *Man!*, May 1936.

18   "Anarchy on Trial in United States Court," *Man!*, January 1938; "Deportations Hysteria," *Man!*, October–November 1936.

19   "Deportations Hysteria," *Man!*, October–November 1936; "Another Refugee," *Man!*, November 1939.

20   "Deportations Hysteria," *Man!*, October–November 1936.

21   "Ferrero Loses Deportation Plea," *San Francisco Chronicle*, February 2, 1937; "Former Publisher Reported a Refugee," *San Francisco Chronicle*, October 21, 1939; "Deportations Hysteria," *Man!*, October–November 1936; "Another Refugee," *Man!*, November 1939; author's interview with Audrey Goodfriend, January 4, 2009.

22   The controversial literature was a copy of *A Revolutionary Anthology of Poetry* that Graham had edited.

23   Now virtually unknown, at the time Aurora Alleva was a very prominent anarchist presence in more-militant, New York and Philadelphia–based Italian-American anarchist circuits during the 1920s and 1930s. She was a popular public speaker and contributor to the anti-fascist, Galleanist periodical, *L'Adunata dei Refrattari* and was also known for her perspectives on anarchist education and parenting. As is well documented, women were often forced into ancillary roles in these anarchist milieus, making her public visibility all the more notable. Even still, and perhaps because of the dismissive historical treatment of anarchist women, there is very little available information about her. Alleva was deeply involved in the defense work, eventually serving as secretary for the Ferrero and Sallitto Defense Conference in New York and becoming Sallitto's life partner. See Jennifer Guglielmo, *Living the Revolution: Italian Women's Resistance and Radicalism in New York City*, 1880–1945 (Chapel Hill: UNC Press, 2010), 150; Tomchuck, *Transnational Radicals*, 2015; and Zimmer, *Immigrants Against the state*, 2015, 193–194. Hippolyte Havel (1871–1950) was a famous Czech anarchist who lived in New York and was a close friend, and biographer, of Emma Goldman's. Ray Randall and Walter Brooks were pen names for Domenic Sallitto and Aurora Alleva, who were both in New York at that time raising funds for his defense. Marcus Graham, "Autobiographical Note," in Marcus Graham, ed. *Man! An Anthology of Anarchist Ideas, Essays, Poetry and Commentaries* (London: Cienfuegos Press, 1974), vii.

24   "In Retrospect of Current Events: A statement of Facts," *Man!*, August–September 1936;

Man!, July–August 1937. Despite this Graham did not remain overly silent or carefully hidden. Several times in late 1936, his name appears with "Bermuda" next to it in parentheses, as the author of articles in *Man!*. This suggests that Graham went on the lam and sought refuge in Bermuda.

25   "US Government Raids '*Man!*' and Jails Editor Again," in *Man!*, October 1937; "Editor May Evade Deportation Charge," *San Francisco Chronicle*, December 9, 1937.

26   "Anarchy on Trial in United States Court," *Man!*, January 1938.

27   "Writers Assailed by Federal Judge," *New York Times*, June 27, 1939; "Marcus Graham Sentenced to Second Six Month Jail Term," Challenge, July 22, 1939.

28   Marcus Graham, "Autobiographical Note," xviii.

29   "Silence About Birth Thwarts His Deportation," *San Francisco Chronicle*, June 7, 1940; "A 'Philosophical' Anarchist Gets 6 Months in Jug," *San Francisco Chronicle*, June 23, 1940.

30   William Preston, *Aliens and Dissenters: Federal Suppression of Radicals*, 1903-1933 (Chicago: University of Illinois Press, 1994), 11.

31   Preston offers a terrific analysis of the "de-criminalization" of deportation making extradition of unwanted immigrants a bureaucratic process rather than criminal, consequently, not subject to due process and the legal safeguards of a right to trial by jury.

32   The Espionage Act made it illegal to make any attempt to interfere with military operations, including recruitment and the Sedition Act of 1918 forbade the use of any language aimed at criticizing the United States government, its flag, or its armed forces. The act also allowed the Postmaster General to refuse to deliver mail that conveyed language deemed to meet these criteria.

33   Indeed, as Zimmer and other historians and scholars of race observe, in so doing, these policies played formative roles in the construction of whiteness by allowing greater access to citizenship for Europeans, while at the same time, making those from outside of northern and western Europe into second-class citizens.

34   For a general discussion on American immigration see Roger Daniels' *Guarding the Golden Door: American Immigration Policy and Immigrants Since 1882* (New York: Hill and Wang, 2004). For an analysis of anti-immigrant and anti-radical legislation passed during WWII, see Margaret A. Blanchard, *Revolutionary Sparks: Freedom of Expression in Modern America* (Oxford: Oxford University Press, 1992), 159; and Robert Goldstein, *Political Repression in Modern America: 1870 to the Present* (Cambridge: Schneckman, 1978), 245.

35   From the foreword by Howard Zinn in Deepa Fernandes, *Targeted: Homeland Security and the Business of Immigration* (New York: Seven Stories Press, 2007), 15.

36   See Estolv E. Ward, *The Gentle Dynamiter* (Palo Alto: Ramparts Press, 1983).

37   Zechariah Chafee, *Freedom of Speech in the United States* (Cambridge: Harvard University Press, 1941), 327.

38   Goldstein, *Political Repression*, 221.

39   No discussion of immigration and repression in 1930s California would be complete without an examination of Mexican repatriation. For an account of this, see Camille Guerin-Gonzales's *Mexican Workers and the American Dreams: Immigration, Repatriation, and California Farm Labor, 1900–1939* (New Jersey: Rutgers University Press, 1994).

40   Goldstein, *Political Repression*, 220–221.

41   For a full account of the strike, see Starr's chapter "Bayonets on the Embarcadero: The San Francisco Waterfront and General Strike of 1934" in Kevin Starr, *Endangered Dreams*, 84–120.

42   Zimmer, "Positively stateless," 128–158.

43   Amanda Sakuma, "Donald Trump's Plan to Outsource Immigration Enforcement to Local Cops," Atlantic, February 18, 2017.

44   Human Rights Watch, "US: Devastating Impact of Trump's Immigration Policy," December 5, 2017.

45   John Burnett, "Big Money as Private Immigrant Jails Boom," NPR—Morning Edition, November 21, 2017.

46   Jennifer Koh et al., "Deportation without Due Process," National Immigration Law Center, 2011.

47   Ahilan Arulanantham, "Immigrant Children Do Not Have the Right to an Attorney Unless They Can Pay, Rules Appeals," ACLU, February 8, 2018, aclu.org.

48   Adam Liptakfeb, "No Bail Hearings for Detained Immigrants, Supreme Court Rules," New York Times, February 27, 2018.

49   EndIsolation.org, "Immigration Detention Fact Sheet," 2017.

50   For up-to-date information about the trial or to donate to the defense, see defendj20resistance.org.

51   For up-to-date information about the trial or to donate to the defense, see waterprotectorlegal.org.

52   Maria Saccetti and David Weigel, "ICE has detained or deported prominent immigration activists," Washington Post, January 18, 2018.

53   Jeffrey Raff, "The 'Double Punishment' for Black Undocumented Immigrants," Atlantic, December 30, 2017.

54   Sam Adler-Bell, "It's a Police-state Mentality," Mask, 2017

55   Harsha Walia, *Undoing Border Colonialism* (Oakland: AK Press, 2013).

56   "Resisting Attempt to Throttle Freedom of Thought—First public Protest," *Man!*, July–August 1935; Albert Strong, "The Fight Against Deportation of Ferrero and Sallitto," Class Struggle, January 1936.

57   Albert Strong, "The Fight Against Deportation of Ferrero and Sallitto," Class Struggle, January 1936.

58   "On the Revolutionary Battlefront—In the Land We Live In," *Man!*, November-December 1935.

59   Strong, Albert, "The Fight Against Deportation of Ferrero and Sallitto," *Class Struggle*, January 1936; "Deportation Officials' Unlimited Perfidies," *Man!*, February 1936.

60   "US Government Raids '*Man!*' and Jails Editor Again," *Man!*, October 1937; "Editor May Evade Deportation Charge," *San Francisco Chronicle*, December 9, 1937; "Stop the Persecution of Graham and *Man!*," *Man!*, March 1938.

61   "Two Fight Deportation," *San Francisco Chronicle*, October 7, 1937; "Anarchy on Trial in United States Court," *Man!*, January 1938; "Deportation of Sallitto Defeated," *Man!*, January 1938.

62   "Anarchy on Trial in United States Court," *Man!*, January 1938.

63   "America's Conscience Speaks Out," *Man!*, October 1937; *Man!*, December 1937. "The Fight Against Deportation of Ferrero and Sallitto," Class Struggle, January 1936; "Shall These Men and Women be Exiled," *Man!*, December 1937; "Stop the Persecution of Graham and *Man!*," *Man!*, March 1938.

COMMITMENT AND CONTINUITY:
A SHORT HISTORY OF ANTIFASCISM IN GERMANY

BENDER

"They got gloves, they got sticks, they got masks, they got everything: An-TIFA."
—Donald Trump

FIRST, WE NEED A SHORT EXPLA-nation of the term *fascism*. It's important to note that the German Nazis never called themselves fascists. The term came from the Italian fascists and the movement of Mussolini, and although this was the prototype for the German Nazis, Italy was an enemy of Germany during the first World War, and therefore the German Nazis identified themselves as National Socialists. Besides this terminological difference, there are some big differences in their ideology, as well. In particular, in the essence of national socialism you can find anti-Semitism on the one hand and the idea of a "*Volksgemeinschaft*," or blood-and-race-based nationalism, on the other. The term antifascist, however, was used by both Italian and German Communists simply because fascism first began in Italy. In the following discussion, both terms, fascism and national socialism, will be used quite equally, but it's important to make clear that German national socialism is a particular and "worse" political form.

Before we look at the autonomous way of organizing, in general, and of organizing autonomous Antifa, in particular, we have to look at its two forerunners in Germany: the historical *Antifaschistische Aktion* of the 1920s and 30s, and the New Left after 1968.

ANTIFASCHISTISCHE AKTION IN THE FRAMEWORK OF COMMUNIST PARTY POLITICS

The historical *Antifaschistische Aktion* was built in the phase when fascism first became a mass movement and was officially claimed in 1932 by the Communist Party, one year before national socialism took power in Germany. While Antifa's contemporary symbol is a red and a black flag, it was originally two *red* flags, symbolizing a united front between Social Democrats and Communists against national socialism. This unity was necessary, and in fact came much too late. After the First World War and the Russian Revolution, there was a split inside the labor movement into the Communist and Social Democrat parties. The radical wing around Rosa Luxemburg and Karl Liebknecht left and built what later became the Communist Party of Germany (KPD). Directly following the war, they tried to drive the so-called November Revolution of 1918 in the direction of a socialist revolution, which, for the Social Democrats, went too far. The Social Democrats then used the right wing corps to beat down the revolutionary uprising. Thousands of revolutionaries were brutally murdered. Luxemburg and Liebknecht were arrested and shot to death on the night of their arrest, and the dead bodies were thrown in a canal in Berlin. All of that happened under the Social Democrats of that time.

After this betrayal, Communists and Social Democrats remained political enemies, incapable of working together—until the National Socialists came to power. The reactionary forces—and later the National Socialists, of course—blamed both for losing the First World War and dividing the nation. Despite their common enemy, or even because of it, the two primary forces on the left fought against each other instead of fighting together against national socialism because they shared the same wrong analysis. Neither took the mass character of the upswell seriously enough, nor its anti-capitalist orientation, and both saw in national socialism only a symptom of capitalism in its final crisis. Therefore, for them, the main question seemed to be: Who will take over the situation? Who is best prepared for the final crisis of capitalism, the Social Democrats or the Communists?

Because of the split after Word War I into a Bolshevik Communist and a reformist Social Democratic party, but also because of their equally false analysis of national socialism, the Communists called the Social Democrats "social fascists," while the Social Democrats called the Communists "red fascists."

By the time *Antifaschistische Aktion* finally came together in 1932, it was all too late. And although the *Antifaschistische Aktion* initiated by the Communist Party was meant to build a united front, they intended the unification to be under the leadership of the Communist Party and their ideology, which was under the influence of the Stalinist Soviet Union and the Communist International, built after World War I.

There are three points to be learned from the failures of this first historical era:

1. Regarding praxis against fascism, some kind of political unity is needed, be it by a "popular front" with centrists and liberals or in a "united front" with left forces only.

2. This leads to the second lesson, which concerns the false analysis of the main antifascist forces of this time. Fascism can, in fact, be seen as a reaction to capitalism in crisis, but this crisis in not the final one before the rise of socialism. Instead, we must take two characteristics of fascism seriously: first, the mass character of fascism (and its mass basis also in the subalterns and the working class), and second, its own anti-capitalist orientation. Fascism exerts its attraction on the masses precisely through its own form of anti-capitalism.

3. This reaction to capitalism and its contradictions and crisis, however, is a limited form of anti-capitalism. The connection between capitalism and fascism is not that fascists and capitalists simply go hand in hand, or that the capitalists use the fascists politically for their economic interests, or that the fascists simply manipulate the masses or the population. This kind of functionalistic and economic view was a weakness in both the Communist Marxist and Social Democratic analyses.

THE BEGINNING OF ANTIFA ORGANIZING IN THE NEW LEFT AFTER 1968

The real forerunner of the autonomous Antifa is the New Left, which began in many capitalist countries of the West after World War II. The beginning of the so called New Social Movements, from which the autonomous movement of the 1980s would be one result, was "the long year of '68," which in Germany was perhaps best characterized as an "anti-authoritarian revolt." We also have to remember that the "year of '68" lasted much longer than only one year, politically speaking. The movement right after '68 had reached a kind of exhaustion, and they were already asking themselves how to organize a movement in decline.

As often happens in the discussion of organization inside the radical and revolutionary Left, there were two poles: one around the concept of organization and party, the other on self-organization, spontaneity, and movement. The same tension played out in Germany when, after the "moment of the movement" of '68, the 1970s followed a more party-driven orientation. The 70s were the decade of the so-called K-groups, various Communist groups with often large memberships, all aiming to become a mass party. It was like the last episode of the history of Communist parties. When the first episode ended in the tragedy of the party-state, this episode was the farce of Communist groups run by students with no impact on the working class, yet exerting great influence for new forms of politics and new political issues. It was in this context of the K-groups that, in the mid-1970s, the first political actions—and the term Antifa—appeared. The first new generation of Antifa grew from within the K-groups.

But just as the student movement went into crisis at the end of the 1960s and transformed itself in the decade of the Communist groups, these K-groups also went into crisis at the end of the 1970s. The situation split into two different orientations to organizing: the Green Party on the one hand, and the autonomous movement on the other.

AUTONOMOUS ANTIFA OF THE 1980S AND ITS GENERATIONS: REVOLUTIONARY, POP, AND POST-ANTIFA

With the Green Party and the autonomous movement, we see again the two poles: party on one side, and self-organizing, networking, and an explicit politics against all kinds of state apparatus and institutions on the other. Like the radical and anarchist Left in the US, the autonomous movement of the 1980s in Germany was organized around squats, autonomous and self-organized youth centers, and independent, non-commercial infrastructures like infoshops, leftist book stores, and other sites of subculture. This model of politics was based more on the plenum and consensus than on decision-making through voting and by majority. Politics functioned more by events and campaigns than by following a program or single theory. The movement was more interested in practical action than in theoretical debates, and it was, generally speaking, more a lifestyle-driven youth movement than an organized and well-reflected intervention in the political discourse.

"THE REAL FORERUNNER OF THE AUTONOMOUS ANTIFA IS THE NEW LEFT, WHICH BEGAN IN MANY CAPITALIST COUNTRIES OF THE WEST AFTER WORLD WAR II."

The autonomous style of politics pioneered not only the organizational styles of non-hierarchical, non-dogmatic, and project-based networking (what could be considered post-Fordist or even neo-liberal organizing), but also the themes and issues of struggle were somewhat decentralized and widespread. Anti-war, anti-atomic energy, squatting and struggle for autonomous free spaces, punk music and independent labels, anti-imperialism, and solidarity for political prisoners were all part of the work. Anti-fascism was only one of these issues, and not the most important one. Also, the fascist movement in the 1980s was very weak, and there was still something like a left hegemony among the youth.

All this changed at the end of the 1980s. Like the student movement of '68 and the K-groups at the end of the 1970s, the autonomous movement also lost momentum at the end of the decade.

In general, one can understand the autonomous movement as a kind of (self-) critique of the Fordist era, the attempt to overcome it and with that part of the movement into post-Fordist ways of working, living, and making politics. The crucial terms, and the attitude of politics and lifestyle in the radical Left were principles like self-determination, self-realization, autonomy, the critique of all forms of authoritarianism, the deconstruction of all forms of representation, and a general resistance against the state and the classical political parties. Some of these critiques have become part of the neo-liberal mainstream; some have been overtaken by anti-capitalist forms of populism; some have been adopted by the neo-liberal "self-improvement." In any case, the autonomous movement had to change with the neo-liberal, post-Fordist, and finance-capitalist flexibility and individualization of society, and the restructuring of the state, with its withdrawal from social welfare, social infrastructure, and an active labor market politic.

On top of these broader changes, there were a number of particular reasons for the exhaustion experienced by the autonomous movement at the end of the 1980s, which laid the groundwork for its evolution:

★ Social ghettoization;

★ Poor public relations and media-politics;

★ The mainstream acceptance of some autonomous and subcultural lifestyle practices: due in part to a new neoliberal form of governance;

★ The crisis of the so-called civil society;

★ The decline of the various *Teilbereichskämpfe*, or struggles on various single issues like opposition to war or to nuclear energy;

★ The implosion of real socialism and the collapse of the Berlin Wall, which changed the situation worldwide; and,

★ New laws created especially against the movement, for example those directed against militant demonstration and the black bloc.

It was in this context that the question of how to organize arose again. This was discussed in the autonomous movement and posed from one of the first and most exposed autonomous antifascist groups, the *Autonome Antifa* in Göttingen, but also by the Berlin group For a Leftist Current (FelS), which initiated what became known as the "Heinz-Schenk Debate."

The organizing debate refers on the one hand to the very dogmatic theory and praxis of the K-groups in the 1970s and tighter organization in general, and on the other hand, the problems and the strengths of autonomous self-organization of the 1980s. The main problem seems to be the lack of commitment and the unaccountable or non-binding character of the structures. They weren't really structures, but rather informal *connections*, officially non-hierarchical, but with internal and very informal hierarchies.

Another problem was that the movement had no continuity on a personal level. It always depended on enthusiastic, experienced, young organizers who would exploit themselves for the movement for a certain period, and who could live an autonomous lifestyle. In other words, there was no place for people with children and family or with a 40-hour-per-week job. This problem only intensified in the 1990s with the advance of the neoliberal restructuring of society.

Together with this lack of structure and lack of personal continuity, there was no continuity on the level of content. There was no transmission of experiences from one generation to the next, and although there were lots of endless discussions, they did not necessarily contribute to theoretical development. The same discussions were repeated over and over, and if anyone wanted to engage in theoretical or critical debate—like about political economy or capitalism on an abstract, systematic level—they had to search for it somewhere else.

In short, the keywords in the debate were *Verbindlichkeit und Kontinuität*, commitment and continuity: there was the need for continuous and binding structures. The most important step was to get organized in fixed single groups with regular meetings, a common basis of understanding, common goals, a clear name, approachability for others, and a capacity and willingness to build and maintain alliances; we needed groups that represented their positions in public via a regular practice that was open for participation.

Another important point was temporary alliances with other groups outside the autonomous movement, like trade unions, the Green Party, the youth organization of the Social Democrats, and so on. But as important as these alliances were, equally crucial was the necessity to maintain our positions and our forms within these alliances, to have—at least on a symbolic level—an autonomous standpoint and a radical expression, like using black bloc tactics at demonstrations.

This leads to another point: we needed better public-relations and a concerned media politics, which meant not really working together with the mass media, but using them to produce optics for the public, which nowadays has become a "politics of the spectacle."

Concerning all these important points—fixed groups on a common basis, media politics, politicizing the youth, making alliances with reformists, having a concrete praxis—for all these points the best topic seems *antifascism*. We have to remember that autonomous politics were always conceived around concrete struggles like squatting houses or resistance to war or nuclear power production, etc., but the idea was always to fight for *more* and to use such politics to politicize people and to radicalize both the struggles and the people who were already involved in them. Antifascism was one of these struggles that stood for anti-capitalism, anti-imperialism, and an anti-state orientation, in general. It was one important issue the autonomous movement had in common that could be the starting point for alliances with others, organized around concrete events like blockading fascist demonstrations. A lot of people who perhaps would have been part of the autonomous movement in the 1980s are now organized in antifascist groups inside of what was left from the autonomous scene.

These groups were usually internally organized in working groups with different issues, even if all the politics happened under the common term *Autonome Antifa*. The idea was still to use one single issue and one single struggle to stand for a critique of capitalist society in general, and to radicalize other people and the larger political context via Antifa. Discussions within this framework led not only to a new style of politics in single Antifa groups, but also to an attempt at a broader kind of organizing.

The two tendencies in tension within the discussions about how to organize were also found in the debate about broader organizing. The conflict was, in short, the question: "organi*zation* or organi*zing.*" The groups that advocated the building of a nationwide organization between Antifa groups initiated the so-called *Antifaschistische Aktion/Bundesweite Organisation,* AA/BO. The AA/BO started in 1992 after a big meeting with a lot of interested autonomous groups as well as a lot of critics. One result of these critiques was the more network-based meeting, *Bundesweites Antifa Treffen* (BAT), which started two years later as a reaction from those who saw the same need to organize but wanted to take other forms. While the AA/BO was focused on a common praxis and unity under already well-organized antifascist groups, BAT emphasized openness and a more platform-based and discussion-oriented style of organizing.

The common goals inside the AA/BO were to take revolutionary and anti-imperialist antifascism as the common praxis. The short-term goals were to build an infrastructure for a nationwide organization with a common program, especially in the form of campaigns organized and coordinated together.

One important point is that anti-fascism initially was chosen not because the fascists were strong at the time; it was chosen for political reasons. Among all the various issues of the 1980s, antifascism continued to feel vital and strategic. It was the best way to politicize younger and mainstream people, to radicalize the already politicized, to receive mass media coverage, to organize concrete actions, and to legitimize a certain level of militancy. It also presented an opportunity to be radical in theory, broaching the connection between capitalist crisis, a socialist alternative, and the option of a fascist "solution."

However, these theoretical and strategic considerations where overwhelmed and run down by the implosion of the "real socialist" states and the East German GDR and the process of German re-unification. In the early 1990s, this ushered in a general climate of nationalism and an enormous boost of fascist groups, fascist attacks, and actual pogroms. The attacks resulted in dozens of people killed, and so Antifa then became a question of self-defense, in particular in the former GDR, where the situation is still much worse today. This general climate and the necessity of self-defense in the beginning of the 1990s, which we called *Die antifaschistische Selbsthilfe organisieren* ("organizing antifascist self-help"), is quite similar to the situation in the US right now with Donald Trump.

Along with their approach to organizing, Antifa meant always more than fighting against Nazis and their infrastructure. Apart from the fact that most Antifa groups worked on different issues (like the autonomous movement before), actions under the name of Antifa were also key for anti-capitalist politics in general and had a militant and revolutionary attitude. Thus, this generation of autonomous Antifa of the 1980s and 90s is considered "revolutionary Antifa."

So, while the first generation of Antifa came from inside the K-groups from the mid-70s to 80s, the second generation was developed within the autonomous movement from the mid-80s on, which has defined its subsequent revolutionary attitude. We can further differentiate the two next phases or generations of Antifa politics again with a decade each. The third generation we could call "Pop Antifa." "Pop" simply means that cultural forms became more important and replaced the old autonomous style: sports clothes, techno acts during demonstrations, stylish layout and outfits, using new technologies like computers and the Internet, working out and being in good shape were all part of the scene and the practice. It was not only a new look, but also a new attitude, a desire not to take Antifa not too seriously; Antifa is necessary and always right, but the Pop period from the mid-90s until the middle of the following decade showed it can be cool even if it's not directly revolutionary.

The fourth generation, the period in which we are now, is not "pop," but "post-Antifa." "Post" means that, while the connection is still there—nothing new or different has replaced Antifa—the actual politics don't really run under that label any longer. The political work is more about organizing, also organizing theoretical debates about capitalism, crisis and precarity, about commons and communism and so on. These groups are often also called post-autonomous.

Perhaps there is a "fifth generation" or phase. Somewhat unintentionally, Antifa has become an international label for this kind of politics outside Germany, as well. Now you see not only the symbol and the slogan everywhere in Europe but in the US; comrades in other countries also see the need for this form of antifascist engagement. Perhaps Antifa is now happening more outside Germany than within.

THE CRITICAL CORE OF AUTONOMOUS ANTIFASCISM

Regarding the theoretical and strategic considerations of Antifa in Germany, it is important to emphasize that while antifascism is fighting against fascism on the streets and in the parliament, it is not a reaction to what fascists are doing. One reason for this is that antifascism is criticising the conditions behind fascist ideology, so it is a critique of the capitalist mode of production, its contradictions and crises, but—and this understanding of fascism differs from the tradition of Marxism and party Communism—also of the ideological reactions inside capitalism. The second reason is that, if certain politics against fascists are unavoidable, like counter-protests or reactions against fascist attacks or murders, antifascism has to follow its own anti-capitalist agenda and define its own goals.

We can locate this critique precisely between two blind spots. Antifa addresses the blind spot of both liberal-democratic and traditional Marxist analyses of fascism. In the end, both have the *same* blind spot: Why does an enlightened modern society, even a liberal democracy, turn into its opposite, into fascism, war, mass murder, and extermination?

Democrats and liberals and mainstream society can only address this tendency as if it comes from outside. Their key terms therefore are extremism, radicalism, and totalitarianism. The democratic identity can only externalize, and maybe *must* externalize, its own immanent turn to fascism as something that comes from outside and happens like a foreign "other"—while it is in fact nothing other than liberal democratic capitalism itself. This is how liberal democracy makes its own inner logic its very own blind spot, while Antifa is based on the insight and the experience that the masses who join fascism are coming from precisely mainstream society. Simply put, if things become critical, the democrats and liberals of today can become fascists.

Marxism sought to reconcile this but failed by delegating the interest of the capitalist class to the fascist party. Marxism ignored fascism's mass character, not understanding that fascism maintained for the masses a true and quasi objective class interest, which is ultimately betrayed and manipulated by fascist ideology. For Marxists, the masses' class interests can only be addressed by Communist politics. Traditional Marxism ignored the mass character of fascism in its epistemological, ideological, and psychological dimensions. It hence has no adequate understanding of the irrational or corrupt economic dimension in fascism, which again is the blind spot of how economic rationality can turn into its opposite, into mass destruction and even in a holocaust. This may not follow a pure economic exploitation or interest, even though it still has to be explained by capitalist categories.

To understand this blind spot of both poles, the Critical Theory of the Frankfurt School was very important for Antifa in Germany. Like Antifa, Critical Theory located its critique in critical distance from both liberal democratic and traditional Marxist theory. For example, Moishe Postone's analysis of anti-Semitism in Germany was very important in the 1990s, especially by analyzing abbreviated, short-sighted forms of anti-capitalism, which we could call a structural anti-Semitism.

In particular, the discussion around the importance of anti-Semitism and nationalism (one outcome was the so called Anti-Germans) in the 1990s was not only important for the understanding of national socialism. It also turned around the understanding of capitalism in general, which is not only problematic by its "normal" crisis, exploitation, inequality, and so on, but by the ideological mass reaction to this. So, in a way it was necessary to defend capitalism and democratic standards against attacks by incomplete forms of anti-capitalism that opposed a productive and useful labor against a finance capital, in which was seen a Jewish principle.

But still—the real object of critique and duty for autonomous antifascists is the inner connection between capitalism and fascism and other authoritarian forms of politics, and the turn from liberal democracy into its own other. The same goes for other forms that the radical Left is criticizing, like we have in identity politics. The connection between capitalism and sexism, racism, anti-Semitism, homophobia, and so on needs to be made explicit. To critique all these inner connections to capitalism on a theoretical and practical level is, in the case of Antifa, the most urgent task. Here the connection of capitalism with repressive and authoritarian forms is not only more drastic, but different ideologies like racism, sexism, nationalism, and homophobia overlap.

The limits of this antifascist critique are the same as in other issues. People freely admit that fascism is bad, and so are other forms of oppression. But they insist that liberal democracy, law and order, the state and its institutions, discussion, and education can protect us. Capitalism is not responsible for these forms.

And that's all true. And nevertheless, we must insist that we can't talk about these forms without talking about capitalist forms and how they, besides its "pure" economic inequality and associated problems, also produce ideology. And, we must use this "pure" capitalism to criticize its abridged, ideological forms of anti-capitalism like in national socialism or in right-wing populism. So, our critique of capitalism is also that it produces its own abridged ideological understanding. The devastation of neoliberalism is not only economic, but is also social, and the immiseration and the poverty that capitalism leads to today is, in our societies, less economic, but more social, cultural, and political.

To summarize, it's not an exaggeration to say that, in Germany more than in every other country, the latest generations of the radical left were politicized by the two political issues, a "normal" anti-capitalism like in other countries, and by the particularity of national socialism and the Holocaust, interpreted from the radical Left as one reactionary answer of capitalism inside capitalism, an anti-capitalist revolt or even a revolution inside capitalism itself. But national socialism was also a total failure of the working class as well as of the population as a whole, creating in the German radical Left a great distrust against any forms of populism, nationalism, and short-sighted anti-capitalism, together with a consciousness of the importance of anti-Semitism not only for the whole idea and ideology of national socialism, but for the way in which capitalist modernity and its crises were "resolved" by masses or at least main parts of the population in fascist countries.

The one lesson we always have to keep in mind is: We can't be safe! Democracy and the population, however liberal they might be, can be something totally different tomorrow, should the conditions arise. There is no protection. If not for our engagement, no one will do it for us, not the police, not the secret service, not the parliament, and not all the democrats, because we can't be sure what they will be or do when economic growth stops, when a rich and well-situated country like Germany goes into a crisis or state of emergency. We should be aware that it is more likely that the masses, including the liberal democrats, will go instead in an authoritarian, populist, racist, nationalist, fascist direction rather than in a socialist or progressive, emancipatory one—just as has already happened in Turkey, Hungary, Poland, in the Middle East after the Arab Spring, and, of course, here in the US.

To be clear: of course, the democratic state and its institutions are something totally different than fascism in power. And of course, there is repression and also *effective* repression against the various forms of fascism by the state. But there is no need to be confused, as it is exactly this repression that turns out to be the problem: the state can only see and treat fascism as a criminal problem and something that comes from outside. It never enacts repression as an antifascist state or with an antifascist identity or constitution, nor can it act against the capitalist conditions. The same goes for every single element in the state-apparatus: police, secret service, public ministers, and mass-media. Of course, they all are against fascists and fascism, but neither as anti-fascists nor embedded in a critique of capitalism. In short, there is no antagonism between fascism and liberal democracy.

This relationship between Antifa and liberal democracy can be brought to the point with one simple quote. When, after the second World War and the victory over national socialism, the German parliament spoke about the *Grundgesetz*, the new German constitution, a member of the Communist Party (which was banned a few years later) said, "Today we do not vote for the new constitution. But one day, we will be the ones to defend it."

CULTIVATE RESISTANCE

Art by Luke Thomas | Justseeds.org

at Saved the World

DIRECT ACTION
FOR KIDS

KEVIN DOYLE

WITH AN INTRODUCTION
BY MAIA RAMNATH

INTRODUCTION

IN HER BOOK *STAYING WITH THE TROU-ble*, wise earthling and "multispecies feminist theorist" Donna Haraway counsels us that the key to collectively surviving our catastrophic times is to look neither to a distant future—whether "apocalyptic or salvific"—or to a mythologized past. Rather, it is to *stay here*, conscious and creative, deeply enmeshed in a present thick with mortal lives and messy meanings, remaining symbiotically intertwined, in murky embrace, with all the other chthonic beings—the tentacular critters of earth. She calls this the "Chthulucene." With these relatives, she suggests, instead of seeking transcendence, we might seek continuous ongoingness, in places damaged by an age of capitalism, colonialism, plantation-system agriculture, and carbon-extractive industry.

Suggesting possible pathways through and beyond planetary devastation—that is, from Anthropocene (or Capitalocene) to Chthulucene—Haraway guides us through the entangled threads of some examples of present-day "sympoiesis" (making together). These are scenarios in which "the sustaining creativity of people who care and act animates the action,"[ii] wherein the boundaries dividing human/animal, art/science/action, and body/biology/technology/ecosystem begin to erode. She urges us to study and practice "humusities," not humanities, and to weave kinship among all the "Children of Compost," as she names the more-than-human terrestrial community of "The Camille Stories," a collaborative work of speculative figuration exploring a beautifully revitalized possible alternative future (of symbiosis with migratory butterflies).

Camille, meet Kevin Doyle. His alternate account of a campaign to save a windswept Irish peninsula from development as a luxury golf course, defending access to the terrain for all locals, strikes me as eminently Chthulucene.

Starting in 2001, organizers challenged this new enclosure through an escalation of creative direct actions on the land. Though the protests were defeated, Doyle and artist Spark Deeley turned the setback into a teachable moment for activating reflection and reimagination, a pragmatic stepping stone to enable hope and future struggle. That is, they created a book for kids. In *The Worms that Saved the World*, a community of feisty invertebrates, realizing they can't save their threatened coastal home in isolation, join forces with the other birds and beasts with whom they share it.

Similar to Doyle and Deeley, Haraway observes that "[o]ne way to live and die well as mortal critters in the Chthulucene is to join forces to reconstitute refuges, to make possible partial and robust … recuperation and recomposition, which must include mourning irreversible losses;" of which there have been many and will be more.[iii] She also reminds us that "[a]ctual places … are worlds worth fighting for; and each has nourished brave, smart, generative coalitions of artists/scientists/activists across dangerous historical divisions."[iv] And finally, "[t]he Children of Compost insist"—and who better to represent Children of Compost than heroic worms?—"that we need to write stories and live lives for flourishing and for abundance, especially in the teeth of rampaging destruction and impoverization." Such a story can be "a pilot project, a model, a work and play object, for composing collective projects, not just in the imagination but also in actual story writing. And on and under the ground."[v]

—MR

1 Donna Haraway, *Staying with the Trouble: Making Kin in the Chthulucene* (Durham, NC: Duke University Press, 2016).

2 Haraway, p. 5.

3 Haraway, p. 101.

4 Haraway, p. 98.

5 Haraway, p. 136.

The Worms that Saved the World

Kevin Doyle
and Spark Deeley

DIRECT ACTION FOR KIDS

Q: Where is a good place to begin? A children's storybook emerging out of a campaign that ended in defeat? How? Why?

A: A few reasons. First off, like so many campaigns and struggles that we are involved in, we lost but we shouldn't have. What I mean is that justice was not done. Rather, we lost because the other side had deep pockets and they also had the police and the state on their side. They didn't win because they were right or because that position had more validity than ours. Our campaign was a classic example of might winning out over right. So, I suppose, our book is a way of saying, "We're not done here, actually."

Q: Perhaps you could tell us something about the campaign that inspired the book?

A: Sure. It was a campaign that happened here in Ireland at a location called the Old Head of Kinsale. It's a beautiful promontory of land with walking trails, bird sanctuaries and magnificent views of the ocean and the surrounding coastline. It has been a traditional walking destination going back through the generations. For generations the land there was farmland with these wonderful walks around and at the edges of it.

Then in the late eighties, the entire headland was purchased by a millionaire developer who had this dream of building a luxury golf course there. He wanted it to be exclusive, too, just for those who had a lot of money. He was aiming at the top end of the golfing business—where luxury intersects with exclusivity and unparalleled scenic position.

A campaign got underway. Many people wanted to preserve the headland as a public amenity, and these developers wanted to effectively privatize it. Our campaign—called Free the Old Head—emerged to take on the developers.

Q: How did the campaign develop and evolve?

A: In truth it was always going to be an uphill battle to win against a determined group of developers. We were up against people with lots of resources. Essentially the campaign took the shape of a series of mass trespasses whereby people went to where the golf course was and insisted on their right to walk onto the Old Head of Kinsale. It was direct action, and, at first, it was very difficult for the developers to stop the protests because they were large and defiant.

Eventually the developers went to the Irish courts, took on the Cork County Council and Ireland's Planning Board, both of which opposed the restrictions on the public's right to walk in the area. In the courts the developers made many outrageous claims and tried to suggest that "the entire right to private property in Ireland was in dispute." Mad stuff. But the courts, well, they sided with the developers. Surprise, surprise, right?

As soon as they did, the Irish police—the Gardaí—rowed in to enforce the rule of law. It was touch and go after that. We really needed more public support and it didn't arrive. So, in the end, public access was lost.

Normally defeat spreads dejection, and in our case there's no doubt that was the case too. But it was really a highly spirited campaign, despite losing. A lot of people mobilized. There were some really big protests. People scaled walls and climbed big wire fences. There was a strong element of direct action mixed in with what were called "People's Picnics," which were very family friendly.

Q: Why a children's book? Why that angle?

A: A few reasons, really. I suppose from the purely practical point, there's a lot of creative space within fiction writing. Even more so in children's fiction. It struck us that the fight at the Old Head of Kinsale was in some ways a metaphor for our times. It was a conflict involving the public good up against private greed. On this occasion privilege and greed won out, but we have to remember, too, that this cannot continue to be the case. We must start to win. The "public good" must begin to win out against privilege and greed. We cannot keep losing all these battles. So subconsciously there was a feeling, for me anyway, that I should write about it and imagine the alternative. What happened at the Old Head of Kinsale, moreover, seemed to be perfect material to bring back to life in an imaginary way. So in our book, the story is carried forth by a community of earthworms. They live on an imaginary headland—on Ireland's Atlantic coastline!—that is invaded by a luxury golf course development. Pesticides and insecticides are used on the land, and soon the worms are getting sick. However, they are rebels, and they speak up. They ask for consideration. The result is that the developers try to eradicate them. The earthworms make a valiant escape, but they know they have little hope on their own. A seagull—normally one of their predators—helps them, and this is how they make their grand breakthrough. They realize that they need to get help, so they set off to tell their story. They build a movement. … We won't tell you the end, but they do win!

The book is aimed at children, but adults really get it, too. It's nice to imagine winning. Another reason why a children's book seemed ideal was that children don't like injustice. When you talk to children about saving the planet from greed, you really are pushing an open door. And we want to tell a story that is optimistic about the possibilities ahead—even though they can sometimes appear bleak.

I guess, when we tell stories or sing songs about injustice and fighting back, we are in part administering therapy and in part defying the impact of defeat. Stories and songs are resistance and therapy.

Q: But the book is primarily aimed at kids?

A: Yes. Most definitely. It is an illustrated book in the best sense of that word. The artist who created the illustrations, Spark Deeley, did a wonderful job. The illustrations have a lot in them, and within some there are more stories—like the one where the worms have a mass meeting.

Also, the story is dramatic. The worms have to fight to survive. It's an adventure and they make it through in the end. So it's an adventure book, too. It is fair to say, though, that it is an "alternative" adventure book. I suppose it fills a gap in the book market. That was another side to why we chose to do a kid's book.

Many activists are parents or will be parents or child-minders at some point in their lives. While the campaign to Free the Old Head was ongoing, I had young daughters myself. I'd be the first to say that there are some really great books out there, but there is a dire lack of books like ours about subjects like this.

Q: You mentioned a few reasons?

A: So many story books reinforce and uphold traditional values. This has been exposed in recent times around gender roles in particular. The video "The Ugly Truth about Children's Books" is a great example. It's on YouTube and well worth a look. A mum and her daughter remove books from a bookcase using the following criteria: Is there a female character? Does she speak? Do they have aspirations or are they just waiting

for a prince? In the end there's not a lot of books left for the mum and daughter to read. One bald fact tells you a lot: 25 percent of five thousand books studied had no female characters at all. For a range of children's media, less than 20 percent of products showed women with a job, compared to more than 80 percent with respect to male characters. So around gender roles, we can clearly see biases in operation. Do these biases help in perpetuating a whole range of disparities that women and girls suffer in society? Of course they do. Conservative socialization is all around us and is dominant in so many spheres of life.

Moving away from gender temporarily, why would we be surprised if there were similar biases around topics like poverty, exploitation or challenging authorities? Of course there are. So in another way, in responding to what happened in our campaign in Cork, we are also addressing other issues not actually disconnected from our general struggle against injustice. People are passive and accept injustice often because they are socialized from a young age to be that way. We need to broaden the scope of radical ideas and alternatives. The area of young children's fiction seemed an obvious place, in a way—and also an important place. Children matter, and they listen and question. We want to link up with that, I suppose.

We've described our book as "direct action for kids," and that's what we think our young citizens should know more about: in life, to be effective, direct action works.

Q: In the promo piece, you say, "a book for adults too," right? Can you talk about this?

A: Adults can clearly see the simplicity of the story. It is a bit of a good-versus-bad tale, and none of the dreadful complications of adult life are really there. But adults like the idea of passing on their values to children, and this book offers opportunities for doing that.

Questions arise from any good story. So in our book, community and solidarity become central issues of survival. The importance of standing by people if they are picked on by more powerful people, by bullies if you like, is also part of the story. Children, sadly, are quite familiar with bullies, so this book is able to speak to them about this issue too.

A key anarchist idea is in our story, by the way; in fact, the plot turns on it. This is the idea of mutual aid. Species on our planet coexist, and there is cooperation, but do we hear much about that? Children hear lots about competition and the Darwinian

idea of the survival of the fittest. So again there is room in the story to look at the idea of cooperation and how humans must, in the end, cooperate and respect the value of the environment.

So there's room in the book for adults to talk and explain to children about different issues that arise. Or you can just read it for the adventure and fun of it.

Q: A lot of positivity from defeat, then?

A: Sure. The book is an imaginary celebration of fighting the good fight for justice. In our story—as you can see from the book's cover image—the earthworms are happy rebels. The cover image, by the way, is from a point in the story before the worms have claimed outright victory. So, via the image, we are reflecting on that very important fact that we sometimes overlook: it is important to fight injustice, but it is often fun, too!

Many of us know this at a personal level, in that we meet some great friends in campaigns, and we meet some really decent comrades. But joining with others, taking part, enjoying participatory democracy, we get to live life. So the book is a celebration of rebellion and the rebellious way, too.

Q: Has the book had an impact on the original issue at Kinsale?

A: Locally it has revived interest in the issue at the Old Head. With the passage of time, the loss of this amenity is felt more acutely. There is a sense that the community was "robbed," and in a way it was. Other cases have also emerged. For example, Donald Trump has a golf course that is involved in controversy in another part of Ireland. There is a golf course in Scotland with a similar tale of woe to tell, also linked to Trump, I think. People have told us about other cases similar to ours that are really about the same type of thing: the greedy 1 percent taking away from the public space. So it has brought an awareness that what happened at the Old Head is about a lot more than just something in our locality.

Another interesting aspect has been the positive response from many of the activists from the campaign. They have really helped to promote the book. I think many of them are proud that their fight has been celebrated with a book of its own.

Q: Some final points?

A: A couple that are related, I suppose. Firstly, we have to play the long game if we want to change the world. I know some ask, is there time? Well, we need time, too. There is a war of ideas out there, and neoliberalism is very pervasive. We need to get in there now. Books are one way of doing that because books are powerful. That has been known from time immemorial. So our book, *The Worms that Saved the World*, is part of the long game. We want to influence young people and have them think early on about the idea of standing up for their rights.

But let's go a step further and ask, what do you do about your rights if the authorities and the courts say no? If they say to you that your rights don't matter. Our book goes into that, and it is unequivocal: if you rebel, think about how to win and what winning entails. Educate, spread your ideas, and build support. It's one of the lessons that emerged from losing at the Old Head of Kinsale. We didn't do enough of that before the crunch came in the fight there.

At the very end of our story, the worms celebrate and they say, about their victory, "We did it together." That says it all.

ABOUT THE AUTHOR

The Worms that Saved the World by Kevin Doyle and Spark Deeley was published in May 2017. It is distributed worldwide by AK Press (Oakland) and AK Press (Edinburgh).

Kevin Doyle is a writer and activist from Ireland. His debut novel, To Keep a Bird Singing, *was published in April 2018 by Blackstaff Press (Belfast). At the turn of the millennium, he was active in the campaign to defend the public's right of access to the traditional walkways on the Old Head of Kinsale. That campaign and his daughter Saoirse's interest in garden worms inspired this story. He is also the author of many articles on anarchism and the anarchist tradition, and teaches creative writing in Cork.*

Born in Birmingham, Spark Deeley now lives in Cork, where she divides her time between professional art practice and community art projects. Her first book, Into the Serpent's Jaws, *an illustrated fable, was published in 2007. This was followed by* Do You Remember Me?, *an illustrated audiobook created with musician Catherine Cunningham. She has also facilitated the production of two volumes of art and writing by community groups in Cork:* Knitting for Squids *and* The Light of the Lantern.

Above: Alec Dunn | Opposite: Sarah Farahat | Justseeds.org

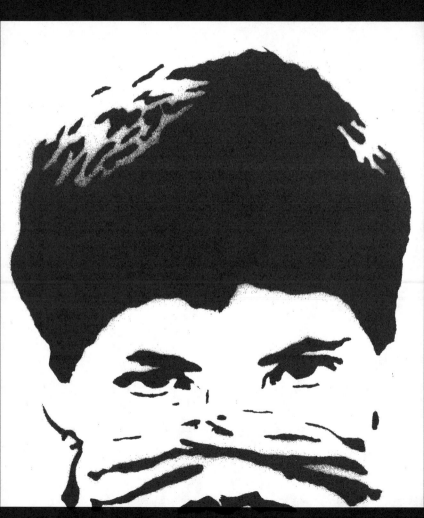

TOYS FOR UTOPIA

ALEXANDER RICCIO

ACCORDING TO HISTORIAN Betsy Hartmann, apocalyptic sensibilities are disproportionately popular in the United States as compared to the rest of the world. Such has constituted what Hartmann describes as the "America syndrome," where puritanical culture and an economy based on militarism feed into the doomsday narrative embraced by this nation's majority population—both historically and presently.[1] Small wonder utopian potentialities are routinely overlooked or dismissed in mainstream political discourse (unless they are the sort of veiled utopianism invoked by Trump's "Make America Great Again" brand of politicking). But where prospects for another world, a better world, are expected to be derided within popular commentary, the abandonment of a utopia on the Left is a phenomenon that does much to constrain our movement energies.

Perhaps the scale of historical Left utopianism has created a sense of futility for such projects, or we've conflated any previous attempts at materializing utopia with a negative quality intrinsic to the conceptual DNA of utopia. Whatever the underlying reasons, confronted with the pervasive common sense that apocalypse is near (or now), the potential for any

« Art by Elliott | Justseeds.org

liberatory movements to succeed today seems to require a recommitment to not only calling for utopia, but to believing that utopia is attainable. If scale debilitates our movements from considering utopia, as so often is the case, my proposition is to begin building our muscles toward accomplishing utopia with a beginner's regime of practice—akin to the exercise James Scott recommends when he writes about performing "anarchist calisthenics" (small scale rule-breaking) on a daily basis.[2]

In this spirit, I've begun to try to imagine how the anti-authoritarian Left might reach into new arenas for prefiguring a "good" utopia, and my imagination has landed on children's toys. Partly this follows from the recognition that within utopian literature, typically so attentive to the socialization of youth, hardly a word is written over what toys a child in utopia would encounter. Sketches of a better society, then, have not sufficiently taken into account the everyday experiences of children. This is unfortunate, especially given the rough consensus of early utopians who believed that children possess tremendous revolutionary potential.

"THOSE PASSIONATE ABOUT SOCIAL CHANGE NEED TO TAKE INTO ACCOUNT CHILDREN'S MULTIPLE SOCIAL REALITIES, IN PARTICULAR THE ARENA OF PLAY."

The next generation, it was commonly held, could propel the future closer to utopian horizons if they were socialized in a liberatory environment. As Murray Bookchin put it, "a social revolution cannot be achieved without the support of the youth, from which the ruling class rvecruits its armed forces,"[3] as well as its general labor supply. I share this optimism about youth, and it appears to me toys are fertile soil for exploring possible futures given that a child's mediation of broader social reality tends to occur through the vehicle of toys, although it would be inaccurate to claim that children are only living lives of play all the time.

If the project of utopia is to "move to the pulse of the concrete," as Ernst Bloch implores,[4] then locating material media through which imaginative capacities are channeled is among the primary tasks. And what better subject than the most imaginative among us; what better objects than the most malleable and interactive?

Yet a strange vacuum exists in discourses surrounding toys—whether it be within social scientific research, feminist blogs, corporate PR, or activist circles—and it seems to me that the lack of a specific inquiry over the potential utopian molding of toys might contribute to larger limitations on political imaginative capacities. Where it is widely recognized that toys in the US today are more gendered than in past decades, and acknowledgements are made over the shaping of children's perceptions through their interactions with toys, still the vacuum exists. Why is no one asking what playthings will look like in utopia?

2016 marked the five-hundred-year anniversary of Thomas More's *Utopia*, and among other limitations of his text, a disappointing feature is More's treatment of children. For More, youth only warrant enough thought to be regulated in numbers and given access to a thorough education.[5] Sad to note, a typical judgment amongst many an advocate is that the "right" education is a panacea for all questions youth-related. Clearly, education is deeply important, but children live beyond the confines of school. As such those passionate about social change need to take into account children's multiple social realities, in particular the arena of play. Toys are simply one component of a child's daily world (at least those fortunate enough to access toys) warranting more attention. As far as critical analysis that actually touches on the subject of toys, the only people willing to tackle the subject seem to be liberal feminists. This has generated a host of excellent critiques over the gender dynamics of toys, pointing to the sometimes subtle and oftentimes overt manner in which gender conformity is inscribed within children's playthings. Such analysis, however, has often been short on ambitious proposals for change, with typical solutions being either short-sighted "fixes" where girls and boys simply mix their toys together, or ones which view the past as a benchmark for better toy alternatives. In this way, go the arguments, boys will be comfortable playing with dolls, and girls will be comfortable playing with action figures, as was supposedly more common at a hopeful moment in the 1970s. In effect, such solutions are calls at the very least to go back to the way toys once looked, and we'll all be happier, or else to get to a point where every parent is comfortable teaching their boys it's acceptable to be a bit more feminine. Consider this *Atlantic Monthly* article's concluding paragraph to an otherwise stellar examination on the gendered aspect of toys:

> Many who embrace the new status quo in toys claim that gender-neutrality would be synonymous with taking away choice, in essence forcing children to become androgynous automatons who can only play with boring tan objects. However, as the bright palette and diverse themes found among toys from the '70s demonstrates, decoupling them from gender actually widens the range of options available. It opens up the possibility that children can explore and develop their diverse interests and skills, unconstrained by the dictates of gender stereotypes. And ultimately, isn't that what we want for them?[6]

Clearly, opening up the imaginative possibilities for children is desirable, and I share the opinion that toys should be decoupled from gender, but what did toys look like in the 1970s which made them so wonderful? Well, you had wild-haired androgynous Troll dolls (described as "so ugly they're cute"), Easy-Bake Ovens, Rock 'em Sock 'em Robots, "Flower Power" and "Disco" Barbie, and, of course, the Six Million Dollar Man action figure. Maybe looking to the past for more gender-neutral toy options is not necessarily the best plan of action for toy interventions (although I will allow that Etch-A-Sketch is a good child's toy).

On the other side of this debate, which the above author criticizes in her closing remarks, is a commitment to the quasi-liberal notion that 'if we just leave children alone to play as they like they'll do fine and discover they might like playing with opposite gender toys on their own' (or you have the more reactionary response that toys *should* be gendered, at the very least so grandparents can know what to buy their grandchildren without getting lost in the labyrinthine halls of Target).

The work done (again primarily by liberal feminists) on toys is extremely valuable, and I do not wish to give the impression that it is anything less; but this work hasn't gone far enough. Nearly all of it centers solely upon the gendered element of toys whereby "fixes" to this issue stray quickly into liberal frameworks of tolerance and inclusivity, without even a fleeting mention of the broader transformative power latent within a child's imagination and potentially stimulated by toys.

Lack of creative solutions, I suspect, follows from the narrowed scope of discourse. It's as if we've all but abandoned the idea of ever attempting to visualize real alternatives, and this is particularly bizarre in relation to toys by the very obvious fact that *toys are manufactured*—we could have direct control over the creation of toys, but we appear to be completely oblivious to this.

Why is the social imagination so constrained within the United States? Could toys perhaps lie at the root of the problem? I wouldn't go so far as to suggest toys are the sole determinant of limited visions, but I do find it fruitful to entertain serious consideration over the role they play within larger reproductive processes. To begin, toys are embedded with a certain capacity to prefigure society. As Roland Barthes wrote, "toys are essentially an adult microcosm; all are miniature reproductions of human objects, as if to the public eye the child were…nothing but a littler [person]… who must be furnished with objects [their] own size."[7] In this respect, I understand the dangers of specifying toys as exclusively manufactured products, not just because this employs a definition of productivity which aligns nicely with capitalist definitional logic but also owing to the clear fact that a child possesses the remarkable ability to pick up a stick and transform it into an elaborate vehicle for play. My intention, however, is to not drift too far from the territory of manufactured and normative notions of toys because it is here that the intervention of human hands is most immediately impactful and therefore appropriate to analyze.

Yet, toys do more than simply representing the adult world infrastructure on a micro level; they do the work of reproducing adult relationships as well. Theodor Adorno and Max Horkheimer remarked that the thrashing of Donald Duck in popular cartoons allows "spectators [to] accustom themselves to [their own beatings],"[8] which they experience in everyday life under capitalism. Social roles inscribed within toys act in an analogous manner, as they prepare children for familiar environments and items they'll encounter as adults. Feminists have been keen in pointing this out for quite some time now, noting the prevalence of toys meant to teach girls how to nurture and care for others while boys simply learn how to punch something as hard as they can—presumably so that the little girl will have some object or another on which to practice her care work.

Roles and norms are ascribed through toys, and this is quite blatant—from army figurines, beauty-standard Barbies, Tonka Trucks, tea sets, and even miniature cash registers where children can practice building their service-sector skills—but less obvious is the slow imaginative conditioning performed upon children through interactions with such toys. As Barthes suggests, "toys literally prefigure the universe of adult functions" in order to "prepare the child to accept them all."[9]

If one were to visit any Toys 'R' Us they would quickly recognize Barthes claim as self-evident. Take, just as one example, the toy set "Paw Patrol," intended for preschool children with their anthropomorphized dog cops, helicopter pilots, fire marshals and other rescue-job characters. The gendering of these toys is immediately obvious as Skye, the female toy, predictably wears pink clothes. Perhaps less obviously important are the depictions of jobs (all of which are working-class occupations). Such toys place within the child's imagination a normative view of available forms of work—hence these jobs become more palatable and less disagreeable to the child who has become "accustomed" to them all. Certainly, the representation of working-class toys (albeit even in dog form) has its own merit, but little wonder that it becomes all the more difficult (or even desirable) to imagine a world without cops when as preschoolers we are playing with toys like Snuggle Up Pup Chase, the lovable and soft dog cop.

"WHY IS NO ONE ASKING WHAT PLAYTHINGS WILL LOOK LIKE IN UTOPIA?"

We should also consider the implications of the pervasiveness of toy cars and trucks. Just think about this hypothetical, and probable, scenario: a child owns a small Tonka Truck. They take their truck on an imaginary trip through the universe they've created in the confines of their own bedroom—one where they drive to the Barbie Mansion, pick up GI Joe, and turn the truck temporarily into a spaceship for a launch to Mars, where they end their play with a fight against aliens with GI Joe at the helm (this is possibly lifted from my own childhood memories). A subtle technique of indoctrination is operating in this instance, quite invisible even to keen observers who would quickly point out the masculinist dynamic of this particular scene. We witness within it a sly familiarization of the child with trucks, and to a certain degree, adult infrastructure as well. Here the child is mapping out a terrain which will become all too recognizable (and unremarkable) upon reaching adulthood, where the notion of mobility accomplished through cars (instead of, say, bicycles) is already deeply implanted within the person's consciousness. It's no secret that Hot Wheels are much more iconic than Finger Bikes, and I feel confident in suggesting that part of the reason we don't put up such a fuss about the lack of public transit or high-speed trains in the US has some basis in our expectations being constrained from the very earliest age.

A child's mind is endlessly creative, but this creation interacts with material objects which have most often been uncritically produced by adults to represent real life. Techniques of normalization narrow a child's imaginative capacities, so that a child who wishes to play house has ready access to all the familiar items which constitute a 'home'—Easy-Bake Oven, tiny couch, imitation cell phone, and plastic vanity piece (typically all pink). These creative moments are subtly inscribed as real-world objects that the child begins to accept as facts of life—and this is precisely where a utopian imagination could intervene. What I am arguing then is that political horizons are shortened by a lack of seriously imagining *different* societal structures, which has a clear consequence in the deluge of boring and constricting toys we find today. Therefore, current toys are in part products of sterile theoretical imaginations.

OPENING THE UTOPIAN IMAGINATION

"Utopia, dream, vision!
So much poetry, so much progress, so much beauty,
yet how much they disdain you!"—Ricardo Flores Magon

Why should utopia be seen as an important concept for liberation? The term is dubious and contestable, so much so that Immanuel Wallerstein prefers his own invented term "utopistics" to specify an intention of examining the real "zones open to human creativity" instead of the problematic "utopias" which in his estimation act as "breeders of illusions, and…inevitably, disillusions."[10] Desiring to break from inherited traditions is understandable, but considering the long history of mobilizations in the spirit of utopia as well as utopia's ability to cull the radical imagination, I embrace the challenge of fostering an emancipatory usage of the term instead of some sleek modification of it. Editors of the collection *Keywords for Radicals* point out that "radicals are left in the difficult position of having to *complete or resolve* the words inherited from injustice rather than simply disavowing them in favor of emancipatory neologisms."[11] As such, before running away with the idea of toys for utopia it is necessary to wrestle with the question of what "utopia" means.

A major current within utopian thought, which in my view has generated much present-day discomfort with adopting utopia into radical movements and social analysis, has been "prescriptive" or "blueprint" utopias. Surveying this utopian thread reveals a history where designs for a future society, and the way to transition toward it, tended toward the worship of meta-narratives and linear progress. Refusals to submit oneself to some universal truth (such as that all society rotates upon the class struggle between owners and non-owners) and the blueprint for a better society was perceived as treason (largely amongst orthodox Marxists). Such ideological orthodoxy partially explains the position of philosopher Karl Popper, who argued that the promise of utopia was nothing more than a demand to "dominate or prostrate yourself"[12] for a program which would allow history to develop along the correct path.

Utopia's genealogical trajectory exposes the germ of blueprint attitudes as early as Plato's *Republic*, widely accepted as a proto-utopian document. In it, the ancient Greek philosopher set about articulating an ideal concept of "justice," which for Plato represented an ideal state of harmony within the human condition and the surrounding political environment. It's not much of a surprise that Plato believed the perfect society could only come into existence once philosophers became "kings," or supreme rulers, and he also made some unique comments on the need to properly socialize children so that they could become the subsequent generation of philosopher kings.[13] However, scant remarks are discovered in Plato's text on the need for play within education. Not only was utopia presented as a blueprint, but it was one that demonstrated how prescriptive tendencies slide quickly into totalitarianism.[14]

Leaping ahead many centuries to 1515 CE, Thomas More published *Utopia*—already mentioned briefly—effectively coining the term. However, as Ursula Le Guin remarked, More's "Good Place was explicitly No Place. Only in the head. A blueprint without a building site."[15] For the next three centuries following More, popular figures were not shy to postulate their own views of a 'perfect' society, but they remained guilty of inking societies without any attempt to think of how such a place might materialize. The list of utopian thinkers is long and illustrated, from Francis Bacon to Henri de Saint-Simon (sometimes noted as a founder of sociology), Robert Owen and Charles Fourier. These last three thinkers, incidentally, were targets of Marx and Engels, who charged these men with developing socialist ideas absent the scientific rigor necessary to bring their ideas into reality. Thus, Marx and Engels lumped Fourier, Saint-Simon, and Owen into a derogatory category of "utopian socialism." A representative passage from *The Communist Manifesto* reads:

> Historical action is to yield to their [the utopian socialists'] personal inventive action, historically created conditions of emancipation to fantastic ones, and the gradual, spontaneous class-organization of the proletariat to the organization of society specially contrived by these inventors. Future history resolves itself, in their eyes, into the propaganda and the practical carrying out of their social plans.[16]

The general critique was that the socialism conceived by these thinkers did not consider how the material development of society would generate the revolutionary agents who would bring utopia to earth, nor did they take into account existing technologies which could be used as instruments for revolutionary action. According to Marx and Engels, these writers were really just writing down what they personally *wished* the world would be. They thought they could will such hopes into existence without grounding their ideas in present material conditions, thus dooming utopia to mere wishful thinking. It's important to understand that Marx and Engels believed that once there was enough material infrastructure and production that everyone could realistically have enough goods for their own comfort plus more to go around, then a socialist society would be possible. By this point people (or I should say the proletariat) would be capable of thinking up more practicable ways of getting to such an ideal state, while also being equipped with the tools to do so. *The Communist Manifesto* was in part an attempt to contextualize history and provide a potential roadmap toward a communist utopia. The ten-point platform the authors proposed within the document could lead us in the right direction, as they argued that the accomplishment of these tasks was imminently possible. The tenth provision they laid out called for the end of child labor and establishment of universal education—again, an admirable step in the right direction but limited by its failure to see children as anything more than empty vessels needing incubation. Needless to say, this platform never mentioned toys; perhaps it would have if children had been regarded as active creative agents in the constitution of a new society.

Nevertheless, the *Manifesto* was an important intervention and improvement over the existing uses of utopian thought, but unfortunately Marx and Engels' corrective did not dislodge the blueprint tendency within the utopian imaginary. Indeed, one can find the prescriptive inflection of historical determinism within the *Manifesto*[17] partly contributing to the situation described by Ursula Le Guin where "it seems that the utopian imagination is trapped…in a one-way future consisting only of growth."[18]

Jumping forward again to the twentieth century, the world witnessed the failures of Soviet-style communism, the rise of US empire, the dawn of neoliberal globalization, and the entrenchment of the Thatcherite belief that "There is No Alternative" to capitalist society. Amidst this climate, utopia seemed a long dead and ossified relic of past social dreaming. Partially to blame, in my view (shared somewhat by Popper), is how often utopia took the form of a blueprint during the socialist experiments of the twentieth century.

It is interesting how few "respected" thinkers continued ruminating on utopia after Marx and Engels, often preferring instead to write about utopia's antonymous twin: the dreaded dystopian future. Just consider the number of popular dystopian classics that have been written in the twentieth century—*1984, Brave New World, Fahrenheit 451, The Handmaid's Tale*, etc.—and contrast this with all the popular utopian classics you can think of written during the same century (meaning ones that your parents, aunts, uncles, and cousins can name, not just you and your friends who are deep into the subject). Does Ursula Le Guin's *The Dispossessed* count?

Today we're inundated with dystopian themes. Actually, the most popular movies and some of the most celebrated books are dystopias, such as *The Hunger Games* and *The Road* (*Harry Potter* feels pretty dystopian to me as well). Within social theory, utopian possibilities are largely not being discussed outside of small circles. Instead, people seem more content attempting to locate any small degree of individual agency they can, no matter how oppressive the scenario. Fredric Jameson remarked that it's been said to be easier to imagine the end of the world than to imagine workable alternatives to capitalism.[19] Why is it easy to envision the destruction of society but difficult to dream up the perfecting of it? This seems to me to be precisely the current quagmire: to resort so frequently to doom narratives is to guarantee social paralysis, while to hint that a better world is possible is to be cast aside as another fringe idealist who doesn't understand human nature, how the world *really* works, or pragmatic methods of improving society. All of this is not to claim that social theory should be centered solely around thinking up utopias, but to highlight that the impulse to think it appropriate even to consider utopia has been firmly quashed.

However, another thread of utopianism offers a possible way out of the blueprint tendency, which could perhaps bring utopia back into major dialogues. This is what I refer to as the prefigurative utopian impulse, where the notion of living the change one wishes to see in the world grounds general principles maintained by proponents. Utopia in this vein becomes a living experiment encouraging changes in practices and interpersonal relationships. In order to accomplish these changes, proponents of prefiguration have insisted upon creating institutional models which can rehearse a desired utopia. Examples include communes, cooperatives and intentional communities, as well as various democratic practices within organizations, such as consensus decision-making. By extension, the concern is less how to control the forces of history to usher in a desired utopia, than to figure out how to inject more democracy into every sphere of social life from the neighborhood to the workplace; and, as I am seeking to persuade readers here, to the toys children dream up and play with.

To be sure, prefigurative utopia has its own set of limitations. Adherents typically shy away from formal political power, as existing political forms are seen as inherently corruptible and a coopting force. This almost ensures that utopian experiments remain small in scale and remote from other revolutionary efforts, as more emphasis is placed on creating community instead of mapping out long-term strategies, including the classical Marxist lines of generating a party, seizing power, and fostering mass consciousness. Although this refusal can often strengthen organizational analysis and practice, nevertheless the failure to extend beyond small-scale autonomous zones and local cooperatives harbors a whole host of roadblocks preventing anything touching a wider social shift. Energies become so invested in creating community and re-socializing practices that an eventual slide into insularity is almost inevitable. Additionally, the prefigurative tendency runs the risk of fetishizing subcultures to the extent that, rather than posing a challenge to dominant culture, participants in these isolated utopias create their own forms of internal hierarchy and status undermining their ability to recruit newcomers.[20] The result has been an inability to translate utopian practices into sustained revolutionary momentum, leading to mass burnout in which individuals may entirely withdraw from organizations and general prefigurative practices. Transitional theories toward utopia clearly need more work to resolve these limitations.[21]

Notwithstanding all of the above, dislodging utopia from its prescriptive variant offers possibilities for advancing a version of utopia more malleable for conditions on the ground today, as well as opening up the imaginative spaces necessary for transforming the mundane into the spectacular. Actively prefiguring utopia now to the greatest degree possible, can help bring No Place closer to some place. Instead of creating a blueprint of what this utopia must be, a more constructive approach in my view is proposing an outline of general principles that strive for a world where coercion, oppression, and hierarchy are minimized, and mutual aid and egalitarianism are encouraged. This approach is also one that understands these are always works in progress, and that is prepared to adapt constantly to new circumstances since societies are never in the habit of remaining static. As well, when utopia becomes closer aligned to a practice-based notion of hope instead of a purely theory-laden one, it opens our sights to the transformative implications latent within everyday items—including children's toys.

SOME ROUGH PROPOSITIONS FOR BEGINNING

"Only in imaginary experience…which neutralizes the sense of social realities, does the social world take the form of a universe of possibles equally possible for any possible subject."—Pierre Bourdieu

What will children play with in utopia? I am not so arrogant as to believe that I alone can conceive of a toy for utopia here in these pages. Instead, I'm proposing that collectively conceptualizing these toys is possible, and hopefully this article can be the modest beginning of such an endeavor. Anarchists seem to me a group that would be receptive to this idea, as testified by the documented histories of anarchist experiments with radical pedagogies through Freedom Schools and communes.[22] It's not easy to locate any other projects more embedded in prefigurative possibilities than this one. Toys inherently prefigure society; attempting to shape toys through means of prefiguration seems likely to instigate a positive feedback loop of further prefiguration.

My first proposition for sparking this cycle is to encourage the practice of horizontal learning and respect between researchers and subjects, or between teachers or caregivers and children. This, in effect, requires both acknowledging children as the primary generators of ideas, since their collective creativity will undoubtedly guide and shape any and all inquiry into utopian toys, and accepting that work must be shared so that no single person can be expected to produce a toy for utopia alone.

It's a bit strange that this even has to be proposed in the first place, since most people who have engaged in intellectual labor quickly discover there's not much chance of producing a uniquely original idea that hasn't already been discussed somewhere in social theory or scholarship. It's clear that research of every kind is based in the cumulative work of previous generations. As eloquently expressed by Peter Kropotkin, "there is not even a thought, or an invention, which is not common property, born of the past and the present."[23] Those working within the academy will find these comments particularly true; yet potential and current scholars based in these arenas are still frequently in a position of conducting research or putting forth theses on an individual basis and in private. The thorough neoliberalization of US colleges has instilled capitalism's attitude of competition for its own sake amongst students and scholars alike. For these reasons, we can no longer perceive universities today as potential spaces for democratizing society, but rather as zones of class antagonism. Which brings me to my second proposition: work on toys for utopia must be a project based not in the academy but in community and amongst the children in our own neighborhoods.

As a final proposal, it appears to me that in conducting any study of utopian toys we would be wise to *produce* the toys we develop in embryo through mutual learning with children. A large portion of the distastefulness of toys today resides squarely in the fact that toys are manufactured within a monopolized industry. I think it's fair to conclude that only in such an anti-democratic space could someone have decided to generate the "Girls Only," My Cleaning Trolley toy (colored pink, yet again). Yes, toy manufacturers actually designed a pink mini janitor's trolley with mop, broom, and small cleaning supplies, branded with the large words "Girls Only" on the package. At this point I think the reader will agree that if we want to see better toys in the world, we need to commit to making them ourselves, through a modest display of direct action and assertion of labor power. As well, understanding that capitalism denies many children access to toys (let alone toys in which they can see themselves), any production of utopian toys should be distributed in an egalitarian way.

Here I hope is the rough beginning of a modest proposal to start working toward prefigurative utopian toys. I hope that readers will advance their own set of ideas for how to engage in this effort. Crucial for this project is a belief that since the reproduction of normative values can be inscribed in toys, then the inverse of this must also be true. Fostering notions that a world without racism, sexism, homophobia or poverty is possible can't be that far-fetched an idea. Why can't toys help promote this view? Lastly, this project of utopian toys cannot be content solely with generating gender-neutral or gender-inversed ones, or decoupling gender entirely from play, not because these aren't worthwhile efforts in themselves, but because they do not go far enough. We need toys that can prefigure a *better* society than this—we want toys for utopia.

ABOUT THE AUTHOR

Alexander Riccio is a labor organizer based in Corvallis, Oregon. He cut his teeth in grassroots university-based organizing for increasing the minimum wage. His writing has been featured in the journal antae and by The Democracy Collaborative in their essay competition "What's the Next System?" Among other projects, Alexander is currently collaborating on a project to revive the commons in the Willamette Valley along with a group of co-conspirators that make up the Common Space Collective.

ENDNOTES

1. Betsy Hartmann, *The America Syndrome: Apocalypse, War, and Our Call to Greatness* (New York: Seven Stories Press, 2017).
2. James C. Scott, *Two Cheers for Anarchism: Six Easy Pieces on Autonomy, Dignity, and Meaningful Work and Play* (Princeton: Princeton University Press, 2012).
3. Murray Bookchin, "Listen, Marxist!" in *Post-Scarcity Anarchism* (San Francisco: Ramparts Press, 1971), 191.
4. David McNally, "Utopia," in *Keywords for Radicals: The Contested Vocabulary of Late-Capitalist Struggle* (Chico: AK Press, 2016), 431-437.
5. Thomas More, *Utopia* (London: Verso, 2016).
6. Elizabeth Sweet, "Toys are More Divided by Gender Now Than There Were 50 Years Ago," *Atlantic Monthly*, December 2, 2015, available at http://theatlantic.com/business/archive/2014/12/toys-are-more-divided-by-gender-now-than-they-were-50-years-ago/383556/ (accessed Dec 2, 2015).
7. Roland Barthes, "Toys," in *Mythologies: The Complete Edition in a New Translation* (New York: Hill and Wang, 2012), 59-61.
8. Theodor Adorno and Max Horkheimer, "The Culture Industry," in *Dialectic of Enlightenment: Philosophical Fragments* (United States: Leland Stanford Junior University), 94-136.
9. Barthes, 59.
10. Immanuel Wallerstein, *Utopistics* (New York, New Press, 1998).
11. Kelly Fritsch and Clare O'Connor and AK Thompson, "Introduction," in *Keywords for Radicals: The Contested Vocabulary of Late-Capitalist Struggle* (Chico: AK Press, 2016), 1-22.

12. Karl Popper, "Utopia and Violence," *World Affairs*, vol. 149 no. 1 (Summer 1986).

13. Plato also felt that governance by philosophers was gender-neutral, meaning women could become philosopher kings as well.

14. Plato, *The Republic* (New York: Dover Publications, 2000).

15. Ursula K. Le Guin, "Utopiyin, Utopiyang," in Thomas More, *Utopia* (London: Verso, 2016), 195-198.

16. Karl Marx and Friedrich Engels, "Manifesto of the Communist Party," in *Marx-Engels Reader*, ed. Robert C. Tucker (New York: W.W. Norton & Company Inc., 1978), 497-499.

17. Whether one chooses to interpret the text this way or not, which I personally do not, does not preclude others from viewing the passages subscribing to notions of linear evolutionary stages of society which are deterministic in their presumptions.

18. Ursula K. Le Guin, "A Non-Euclidean View of California as a Cold Place to Be," in Thomas More, *Utopia* (London: Verso, 2016), 172-173.

19. Fredric Jameson, "Future City," *New Left Review* 21 (May-June 2003), available at https://newleftreview.org/II/21/fredric-jameson-future-city (accessed December 31, 2016).

20. For a thorough examination of how counter-cultures develop their own forms of hierarchies, see Nazima Kadir, *The Autonomous Life? Paradoxes of Hierarchy and Authority in the Squatters Movement in Amsterdam* (Manchester: Manchester University Press, 2016).

21. For an excellent overview of prefigurative politics and its limitations, see Wini Breines, *The Great Refusal: Community and Organization in the New Left: 1962-1968* (New York: J.F. Bergin Publishers, Inc., 1982) and Carl Boggs, "Revolutionary Process, Political Strategy, and the Dilemma of Power," *Theory and Society*, vol. 4 no. 3 (Autumn 1977), 359-393.

22. See Paul Avrich, *The Modern School Movement: Anarchism and Education in the United States* (Oakland: AK Press, 2005) and Andrew Cornell, Unruly Equality (Berkley: University of California Press, 2016).

23. Peter Kropotkin, *The Conquest of Bread* (New York: Dover Publications, 2011).

REIMAGINING REVOLUTIONARY ORGANIZING: A VISION FOR DUAL POWER

JOHN MICHAEL COLÓN
MASON HERSON-HORD
KATIE S. HORVATH
DAYTON MARTINDALE
MATTHEW PORGES

« Art by Josh MacPhee | Justseeds.org

TODAY'S POLITICAL SITUATION is a crisis, in which nothing fundamentally changes despite a seemingly endless series of catastrophes. Even in allegedly democratic nations, the institutions that channel national decision-making are structurally incapable of staving off ecological and economic collapse, and securing a decent life for everyone. What we face is a colossal collective action problem.

The German-American political philosopher Hannah Arendt argued that intolerable situations such as ours could be cast aside by the public's revolutionary withdrawal of support from governing institutions. As a prominent theorist of totalitarianism, political violence, and direct democracy, Arendt developed im`-portant concepts that help disentangle the problems humanity currently faces and indicate a way forward.[1]

Power is conventionally understood in politics as the ability to make others do things, often through violence or coercion to enforce obedience and domination. In *On Violence*, however, Arendt demonstrates that power works quite differently in actual human societies. She defines "power" as people's ability to act in concert—the capacity for collective action, and thus a property of groups, not individuals. Leaders possess their power only because their constituents have empowered them to direct the group's collective action.

Arendt argues that all power, in every political system from dictatorships to participatory democracies, emerges from public support. No dictator can carry out his or her will without obedience from subjects; nor can any project requiring collective action be achieved without the support, begrudging or enthusiastic, of the group. When people begin to withdraw their support and refuse to obey, a government may turn to violence, but its control lasts only as long as the army or police choose to obey. "Where commands are no longer obeyed," Arendt writes, "the means of violence are of no use.... Everything depends on the power behind the violence."[2] The understanding that power emerges from collective action, rather than from force, is a key component of our transitional vision.

As a revolutionary political strategy, however (rather than a mere description of certain past political events), Arendt's theory of power requires several modifications. First, without preexisting mass organiza-

"WHAT WE FACE IS A COLOSSAL COLLECTIVE ACTION PROBLEM."

tion, the public has no way to collectively withdraw its support. Individuals acting alone have no impact on the state's power. This is why Arendtian revolutions (Hungary in 1956, Czechoslovakia in 1989, Tunisia in 2011) occur only in exceedingly rare moments of crisis.

Second, most people will never even consider retracting support for governing institutions if they don't see viable alternatives. As Antonio Gramsci explained a century ago, the ruling class's cultural hegemony can be undermined only by what he called a "war of position:" developing a material and cultural base within the working class to craft an oppositional narrative and to organize oppositional institutions.[3] The organization of unions, worker-owned firms, and housing cooperatives is what makes socialism a real lived possibility around which greater movement-building can occur.

Third, withdrawal has serious costs. Even absent violent repression (a feature of even today's most liberal democracies), we are made dependent on capitalist and state institutions for access to basic survival needs and avenues for collective action. Transcending capitalism and the state thus requires having alternative institutions in place to meet those needs and organize people to act powerfully in concert with one another. Retracting support without engaging in such oppositional institutions is rarely distinguishable from apathy.

Fourth, we cannot neglect the preformation of the postrevolutionary society— the need to actively create institutions to replace the ones we have now. Arendt has somewhat romantic notions about the forms of organic democratic politics that will emerge in the vacuum following a mass retraction of public support for governing institutions. To a certain extent, history is on her side. The Syrian Kurds' democratic confederalism in Rojava, the workers' councils of revolutionary Russia and Germany and Hungary, the Paris Commune, Argentina's factory takeovers, and Catalonia's anarchist revolution all exemplify community-rooted participatory politics emerging out of revolutionary crisis. More complex institutional arrangements, necessary to manage and coordinate society as a whole, however, are beyond the reach of spontaneous face-to-face democracy. Far from expressing public will, such institutions are usually seized or assembled by whichever party or faction is best positioned to capitalize on the conditions of uncertainty (as Arendt herself notes).[4] A revolutionary transfer of authority to popular organs of radical democracy requires the pre-existence of such participatory institutions, not a naive faith that they will be conjured into being out of a general strike, mass retraction of public support, or insurrectionary upheaval.

Arendt's analysis of the sources of state power, we contend, generally applies to capitalist institutions, too. These can be supplanted only by creating sustainable egalitarian alternatives which sap the public's dependency on and acceptance of the status quo. An effective political strategy for the present must combine the best of Arendt's intuitions about the workings of power in society and possibilities for popular revolution with an organizing vision of community institution-building.

In early stages, crafting the political infrastructure of radical democracy and libertarian socialism will be mainly local, through outgrowths and codifications of existing social processes that can be expanded into mainstream practice and incorporated into a broader strategy. The community institutions proposed here are modular. They can stand alone as individual projects, fine-tuned to solve specific problems created by the current system's failures, but they are designed to be organized as a network. By working together and mutually reinforcing one another, these institutions can qualitatively change the power relations of a city or neighborhood and lay the groundwork for new macrostructures of self-governance and civil society. Through engineering and managing new institutions of their own, communities can cultivate a creative and communal spirit that will empower them to take control of their lives, connect to one another across cultural and geographic distances, and develop the egalitarian foundations of a new society. Only such a process serves as the basis of a truly democratic ecosocialism.

Over time, confederations of directly democratic councils governing society in parallel to the state could come to challenge it. This situation is what Left-Green theorist Murray Bookchin called "dual power."[5] The section below explores how to build dual power in the here and now by modifying and transcending current approaches to community and labor organizing to create radically democratic community institutions.

II. RULES FOR RADICALS ARE MADE TO BE BROKEN

To bring this vision to life in our own neighborhoods, we need to learn from the successes and failures of existing modes of organizing.

Community organizing in the United States has historically been dominated by a model known as "institution-based community organizing" (or "broad-based community organizing"). This model evolved mid-century out of Saul Alinsky's work in Chicago neighborhoods and the Southern Christian Leadership Conference's civil rights organizing across the South. The legacy of the Civil Rights Movement is obviously central in the progressive political imagination, and Alinsky's *Rules for Radicals* is still used as a foundational handbook for organizing.[6] The central idea of this model is that such community institutions as labor unions and religious congregations are already internally organized and already have community buy-in, making them the perfect vehicle for more powerful organizing in the community's interest. The Civil Rights Movement, for example, was organized through the existing strength of the Black church. Major organizing networks based on this legacy continue to use the methodology of institution-based, largely faith-based organizing across the US, and public interest advocacy organizations draw upon the Alinskyist tradition in their campaigns on many issues.

Institution-based organizing relies on two premises that we question, however. One is that community institutions already exist, ripe for organizing. The other is that representative democracy can still be made to work for the people if only they are engaged and apply enough pressure.

In recent decades, community institutions in America have crumbled under the advance of the neoliberal state, the dismantling of organized labor, the privatization of public space and public schools, the closing of recreation and community centers, and the waning importance of organized religion, especially for younger generations. Simply put, working through today's community institutions does not get us very far if there is a dearth of them and if the surviving ones are less important than they once were.

Using existing institutions to demand concessions from power also violates the influential "iron rule" of the Alinsky-founded Industrial Areas Foundation: "never do for people what they can do for themselves." In institution-based organizing, the iron rule means that professional organizers should emphasize training and leadership development in the community, rather than running campaigns on *behalf* of the community. The former method builds power and grows the organization or movement; the latter stifles it. Although the philosophy behind the iron rule is sound, institution-based organizing does not take it far enough. Training people to apply pressure to the levers of power in a (barely) representative democracy still means ultimately relying on others—mostly unresponsive "elected" officials and undemocratic institutions—to make changes on behalf of a community, rather than initiating those changes themselves.

Institution-based organizing networks and the sprawling ecosystem of public interest advocacy groups also subscribe to another core Alinskyist principle: that the issues they take up must be concrete, immediate, and winnable. In our experience, these strictures have limited the scope of what such organizations consider possible and the extent to which they can change the basic structures of society. Our model likewise emphasizes the concrete practices of meeting community interests and does involve taking immediate winnable steps—but the focus is always on a larger vision of systemic transformation.

Although it should draw upon this legacy of community organizing, the transition beyond capitalism and statism must prioritize building up new communal institutions of democratic self-governance and self-sufficiency rather than working through the traditional organizing model that eschews service provision. Creating and organizing these institutions are means for building the community's power, preparing it to wage more traditional organizing campaigns when needed to force the government or private sector to act in the community's interest. At the same time, these democratic cooperatives can be ends in themselves, filling in the gaps of the shrinking welfare state through networks of mutual aid and direct action where and when the state and private sector fail to respond to citizen needs or demands.

The best US precursor to this is the Black Panther Party. Even so, the full radical potential of its organizing model was left unrealized. Founded in 1966, the Black Panthers articulated a vision of Black Power and revolutionary socialism in opposition to American militarism, the impoverishment of Black communities, and police violence. Their "Serve the People" programs included free breakfasts for hungry schoolchildren, a cooperative shoe factory, community health clinics and education centers, and cooperative housing for low-income people.[7] They often illustrated the programs' function with the metaphor of being stranded on a life raft—the community must take practical steps to stay alive in the present, but never forget that the real goal is to make it to shore, to revolution. The Panthers understood these programs as "survival pending revolution"—a means of sustaining their communities until they could achieve liberation.

> "TRANSCENDING CAPITALISM AND THE STATE THUS REQUIRES HAVING ALTERNATIVE INSTITUTIONS IN PLACE TO MEET THOSE NEEDS AND ORGANIZE PEOPLE TO ACT POWERFULLY IN CONCERT WITH ONE ANOTHER."

Survival programs proved to the community that the Black Panthers were serious about improving Black people's lives. This approach let the Panthers build power where revolutionary rhetoric alone would have failed, and membership swelled. Even so, such programs could have been structured toward building power even more than they did. If they address more than mere survival, by building the structures of a society autonomous from and in opposition to the state and capital, survival programs can become liberation programs as well. By meeting basic community needs, such institutions rupture capitalism's control over people's lives, allowing oppressed people to carve out space within capitalism, defend and expand that space, and thus transform the world around them.

III. REVOLUTIONARY INSTITUTION-BUILDING IN PRACTICE: THE FIRST INTIFADA

To see how institutions of mutual aid and participatory democracy can mobilize society into a powerful resistance movement, we can look to the legacy of struggle in Palestine.

The First Intifada broke out in late 1987 as a mass uprising against the Israeli occupation of the Palestinian territories. It was one of the most powerful popular mobilizations in recent history, largely responsible for the Oslo Accords and the formation of the Palestinian Authority as a framework for achieving Palestinian independence. The flaws of this framework notwithstanding, this popular struggle upended the previous consensus around the *de facto* annexation of the occupied territories and the impossibility of a Palestinian state, changing the course of the conflict forever.

Most discussion of the First Intifada focuses on the role of mass protest in making Palestinian society ungovernable for Israeli occupying forces. Less discussed is the role of community organizations of mutual aid and confederated participatory democracy in making such mass protest possible. The brief overview below shows how these institutions laid the groundwork for and sustained a revolutionary upheaval against one of the most totalitarian political orders of that time.

The prison system became a political incubator of the Palestinian resistance movement and offers a microcosmic example of the development of dual power in the much larger prison of the occupation. With hunger strikes, political prisoners eventually won concessions for their own self-administration within the prisons. They assembled structures of political organization and representation, forced prison authorities to recognize those representatives, and developed a division of labor to attend to hygiene, education, and other daily tasks. Palestinian prisoners described this arrangement as *tanthim dakhili* ("internal organization"), similar to the concept of dual power. Even in the least free of circumstances, these prisoners carved out space for self-governance and created the preconditions for revolutionary struggle.

Prisoners taught and studied everything from Palestinian history to Marxist political economy, often for eight to fourteen hours per day.[8] As these freshly educated and trained political activists were released back into society, the resistance movement was galvanized. Illiterate teenage boys arrested for throwing stones reentered the fray months later as committed, competent organizers who had studied movement building, strategic civil resistance, and dialectical materialism.

Meanwhile, the organizing context outside of prison transformed dramatically. Saleh Abu-Laban, a Palestinian political prisoner from 1970 until 1985, stated, "When I entered prison there wasn't a 'national movement;' there were only underground cells that performed clandestinely. When I got out I found a world full of organizations, committees, and community institutions."[9]

Central to this new world of community organizing was the Palestinian labor movement. Unions were formed out of workers' places of residence rather than workplaces because migrant labor was prevalent and Palestinian unionism within Israel had been criminalized. Unions then formed strong alliances with local organizations in the national movement. With rapid growth in the early 1980s, labor unions found it necessary to decentralize and democratize their structure to become more resilient as Israeli repression intensified against union leaders and organizers.[10] These local unions were networked together through the Palestinian Communist Party and the Workers' Unity Bloc, creating a web of labor organizers and community groups that linked their class struggle to the larger project of national liberation.

Young people also played a vital role. They organized student associations at high schools and universities. There, they assembled demonstrations, set up volunteer committees serving refugee camps and poorer villages, and funneled youth into the national movement. Youth cultivated solidarity practices that were crucial during the uprising, including the formation of a largely student-run national mutual aid network.

The Palestinian women's movement was perhaps the most important of all in laying the groundwork for the First Intifada.[11] These feminist organizers started by addressing their members' real material needs, but deliberately oriented these projects toward the higher goals of women's liberation and Palestinian national liberation. The women's committees they formed brought together housewives and working women in cities and towns throughout the occupied territories. They set up classes and cottage industry cooperatives (managed along roughly anarcho-syndicalist lines, with one vote for each worker-member) for women looking to generate supplementary income.[12] Organizers went door-to-door in the poorer villages and refugee camps to reach women who were illiterate, economically dependent on men, and largely confined to private domesticity. Free cooperative childcare allowed these poorer women to join the co-ops, take literacy and vocational classes, and participate in women's committee politics.[13]

The women's committees were a confederal system, with webs of individual committees democratically operating local projects. Each women's committee nominated a member to represent its members at a district/area committee, which in turn nominated representatives for the national body. These national women's committees built strong ties with labor unions, expanded mutual aid supply lines, and developed community leaders.

Such activities served multiple purposes. They made the conditions of military occupation more livable, sustaining Palestinian families in the face of relentless colonization. They provided individual women with greater economic independence, allowing them to slowly stretch the boundaries of patriarchal control and participate more actively in public life and the national movement. They laid the early foundations of the "home economy," which fostered Palestinian self-sufficiency and later provided the sustaining material support for economic resistance against the Israeli occupation, in forms such as boycotts and strikes. Finally, these women built up the community's organizational capacity to wage a broad-based social struggle drawing on all segments of Palestinian society.

These various local community institutions overlapped with one another cooperatively. Women's committees and voluntary work committees joined forces for many of their charitable projects; feminist organizers ran labor unions for garment workers; and political parties helped link different labor groups together. The labor, student, and women's movements eventually coalesced in the Intifada's most important political institution—al-lijan al-sha'abiyya, the popular committee[14]—and gave birth to radically democratic council management of the community.

When an Israeli military truck killed four Palestinians in the Jabalia refugee camp on December 8, 1987, a mass protest movement rapidly ignited across the territories. Huge demonstrations sprang up in every camp and city, demanding justice for the victims and an end to the occupation. By January 1988, popular committees had formed out of the social infrastructure of local unions, women's committees, student associations, political party organizing, and friendly neighbors across the West Bank and Gaza Strip. Committees carried out tasks for an extraordinary array of social functions: collecting garbage, determining local strike dates, collecting donations through an "alternative taxation system," distributing food and medical aid, repairing damaged buildings, organizing barricade building, developing local economic self-sufficiency, and more.

Like the women's committees, the popular committees coordinated with one another through a confederated structure. Local committees nominated delegates to represent them at area/municipal committees, which coordinated resistance activities among neighborhoods, camps, and nearby villages. These committees in turn elected representatives to a district committee, and district committees sent representatives to al-Qiyada al-Muwhhada, the secret Unified National Leadership of the Uprising (UNLU).[15] The UNLU first began distributing pamphlets in January 1988 detailing strike dates, boycotts of Israeli goods, marches, and other guidance for individual popular committees, such as calls to develop the "home economy,"[16] to withhold taxes from the occupying regime, and to resign from posts in the occupation government.

This structure acted as a democratic confederalist shadow-state, parallel and in opposition to the repressive and undemocratic military government, with enthusiastic nationalist legitimacy and organizational effectiveness to make up for its lack of monopoly on violence. It carried out a three-part strategy of resistance to the occupation: undermining the hegemony exercised by the occupation and its institutions; out-administering the occupation with parallel institutions to meet human needs; and creating a new nationalist hegemony to supplant the occupation.

This organizational structure also proved essential for coordinating local actions into territory-wide coherence. It gave ordinary Palestinians a voice in the direction of the struggle and the formation of their new society.[17] Building dual power from the ground up is what enabled the mobilization of the entire Palestinian public against its collective disenfranchisement and dispossession. For those of us inspired by the rise of horizontalism in today's social movements, the First Intifada has much to teach us about the organizational conditions necessary for this ideal to be truly realized in a practical and powerful way.

Eventually, the scale of repression became too much for even this highly resilient model to bear. The imprisonment of most experienced organizers and the paranoia about the wide network of paid or coerced informants in Palestinian society eventually fractured and then crumbled the Intifada's organizational capacity, and the movement collapsed. How the Palestinian liberation movement could have done better to overthrow the occupation regime is another discussion. The movement nonetheless illustrates how this form of grassroots democratic institution-building can channel collective action on an incredible scale and empower participatory democracy and mutual aid as the guiding forces of a society. The end-goal of the First Intifada was not to build libertarian socialism or radical democracy, but to replace the occupation with a democratic Palestinian state. Even so, a similarly structured movement with different goals could trace an analogous path, with greater success in a freer society like the United States.

IV. A POSSIBLE PATH FORWARD

That path would look something like the following: movements would assemble direct-democratic and socialistic institutions in civil society; coordinate these through a system of decentralized and confederated democratic assemblies, such as neighborhood councils, with a dual power relationship to existing state structures; transform systems of local governance to place these popular confederations in control of the public sphere to encourage the further development of the socialist civil society that made such reform possible in the first place; and further confederate these municipal democracies to create first regional and then eventually global decision-making bodies rooted in bottom-up democracy capable of addressing problems such as globalization and the ecological crisis, transitioning us into a libertarian ecosocialist society.

The path and the system described above are a framework, a way to ensure that the systems to come can represent and respond to the needs and desires of the people who inhabit them. Actually building that world, then, is up to all of us.

For a full blueprint of what building dual power and transitioning to democratic community control might look like in a city today, read the full essay, "Community, Democracy, and Mutual Aid: Toward Dual Power and Beyond"[18]
*Available at **www.symbiosis-revolution.org***

ABOUT THE AUTHORS

John Michael Colón is a writer and journalist based in Brooklyn whose work has been published in *Prelude* and *In These Times*, among other places.

Mason Herson-Hord is an organizer with Motor City Freedom Riders, building power with bus riders in Detroit to win better public transit in the region.

Katie Horvath is an anthropologist and a community organizing trainer working to build neighborhood democracy in Detroit.

Dayton Martindale is an assistant editor at *In These Times* in Chicago and an organizer for animal rights and environmental justice.

Matthew Porges is a PhD student in Social Anthropology at the University of St. Andrews in Scotland.

The authors are co-founders of Symbiosis, an organization working to lay the groundwork for the sort of revolutionary confederation laid out above in communities across North America, the steering committee of which includes John, Michael, Mason, and Katie. Further information at symbiosis-revolution.org.

ENDNOTES

1. Hannah Arendt, *The Origins of Totalitarianism* (Cleveland: Meridian Books, 1951).
2. Hannah Arendt, *On Violence* (New York: Harcourt Books, 1970), 48-49.
3. Antonio Gramsci, *Selections from the Prison Notebooks*, ed. and trans. Quentin Hoare and Geoffrey N. Smith (New York: International Publishers Company, 1971).
4. Some examples: the political opportunism of the Bolsheviks in the Russian Revolution, Ayatollah Khomeini's faction in the Iranian Revolution, and the Muslim Brothers in the Egyptian Revolution.
5. Murray Bookchin, "Thoughts on Libertarian Municipalism," *Left Green Perspectives*, no. 41 (January 2000).
6. Saul Alinsky, *Rules for Radicals: A Practical Primer for Realistic Radicals* (New York: Vintage Books, 1971).
7. David Hilliard, ed., *The Black Panther Party: Service to the People Programs* (Dr. Huey P. Newton Foundation, Albuquerque: University of New Mexico Press, 2008).
8. Maya Rosenfeld, *Confronting the Occupation: Work, Education, and Political Activism of Palestinian Families in a Refugee Camp* (Stanford: Stanford University Press, 2004), 252; Avram Bornstein, "Ethnography and the Politics of Prisoners in Palestine-Israel," *Journal of Contemporary Ethnography*, 30, no. 5 (2001), 546 – 574.
9. Rosenfeld, *Confronting the Occupation*, 218.
10. Joost R. Hiltermann, ed., *Behind the Intifada: Labor and Women's Movements in the Occupied Territories* (Princeton: Princeton University Press, 1993), 7, 34, 57, 64.
11. Joost R. Hiltermann, "The Women's Movement During the Uprising," *Journal of Palestine Studies*, 20, no. 3 (spring 1991), 48-57.
12. Hiltermann, *Behind the Intifada*, 52; Philippa Strum, T*he Women are Marching: The Second Sex and the Palestinian Revolution* (New York: Lawrence Hill Books, 1992), 74-78.
13. Strum, *The Women are Marching*, 53.
14. Also called "neighborhood councils" (or, in rural areas, "village councils").
15. In older sources, the UNLU is commonly mischaracterized as a command structure with political parties at the center. More recent interviews with veteran organizers in the popular committees provide little to no evidence for this framing. Rather, the UNLU was dependent on and democratically embedded in the popular committee network. See Mazin B. Qumsiyeh, *Popular Resistance in Palestine: A History of Hope and Empowerment* (London: Pluto Press, 2011); Mason Herson-Hord, "Sumud to Intifada: Community Struggle in Palestine and the Western Sahara" (undergraduate thesis, Princeton University, 2015).

16. Community gardens, cottage industry cooperatives, food and medicine distribution networks, and other forms of economic self-sufficiency provided subsistence for neighborhoods so they could both provide for all members of the community and participate fully in strikes and boycotts.

17. One First Intifada veteran interviewed in Beit Sahour in 2014 said that he was jokingly accused of being in the UNLU because the suggestions his popular committee had given him to present to Beit Sahour's town-wide committee appeared in a UNLU leaflet two weeks later. This model was extremely effective at disseminating strategies for popular resistance. The idea of a tax strike, deployed so effectively by the people of Beit Sahour, was actually first proposed by the popular committee of a small village near Nablus and ended up in a communiqué printed and distributed by popular committees throughout occupied Palestine. See Herson-Hord, "Sumud to Intifada."

18. John Michael Colón, Mason Herson-Hord, Katie Horvath, Dayton Martindale, and Matthew Porges, "Community, Democracy, and Mutual Aid: Toward Dual Power and Beyond, *The Next System Project*, April 2017.

BEYOND MEDICARE FOR ALL: AN ANARCHIST ALTERNATIVE TO GOVERNMENT HEALTHCARE

SARAH MILLER

« Art by Josh MacPhee | Justseeds.org

WHEN I FIRST MET MARY, she had been admitted to the hospital for the fifth time in six months. Mary was a sixty-seven-year-old woman, a former smoker with chronic lung issues. The nurses joked, "Oh, I guess it's your turn to deal with her." She had come to the Emergency Department again the previous night at 9 o'clock because she felt like she couldn't breathe. In a panic, she called 911.

As I started my assessment, I asked her about her frequent visits. "Hi, Mary! I'm going to be your nurse this evening. So what happened? I saw that you scheduled an appointment with your lung doctor 2 weeks ago?" Yes, she assured me, she did see her doctor. He started her on a new inhaler and gave her samples to try. She felt like the new medication was helping, but when she went to pick up the prescription at the pharmacy, the cost was almost $300 for a one-month supply. So she went back to her old medications and her lung issues got worse once again.

Mary's daughter helped her apply for a patient assistance program through the drug manufacturer, but she was still waiting for a response. Medicare started when she was sixty-five years old, but it did not cover medications unless she enrolled in Part D. Part D is generally managed by private insurance companies like the American Association of Retired Persons (AARP) or Aetna, and entails a separate policy with associated premiums, deductibles and co-pays.

Rodney was another "frequent flyer." A fifty-five-year-old man, Rodney had congestive heart failure, a chronic condition that waxes and wanes, causing periods of significant fluid retention and resulting shortness of breath. To make matters more complicated, Rodney lived alone and had chronic mental health issues. He did not always make it to his appointments and used the ER when he started to feel poorly.

He came to the ER three days after his most recent hospital stay, saying that he felt short of breath. His symptoms were worsening but the doctor advised that Medicare might not pay for another admission as he had just been discharged less than a week ago. He chose to return home, and promised to call his doctor in the morning. When the ambulance crew brought Rodney back to the ER two days later, he was intubated, unable to breathe on his own.

MEDICARE WILL NEVER BE "FOR ALL"

"Medicare for All" is a rallying cry for much of the American Left, but why? Why do we seek out a government-based solution when Medicare has already failed so many? Ethically speaking, a system that provides for more people with fewer obstacles to receiving care is worth supporting. However, the reforms being proposed are still steeped in the status quo of the current capitalist health care system.

Universal health care proposes socialization of consumption, but not of the production or provision of medical services and care. While it may allow some people to have access to free health care, it does nothing to eliminate the fact that insurance companies and government agencies are dictating and directing care. By threatening hospitals and providers with decreased reimbursement for certain conditions, Medicare uses its power and influence to tell doctors how to treat their patients, what tests to run, which drugs to prescribe, and whom to admit to the hospital.

Medicare's reimbursement reduction programs, aimed at lowering the number of cases like Rodney's, exist to save money, not to help patients. In 2014, Medicare fined 77 percent of hospitals that serve lower-income patients—often called "safety-net hospitals"—for readmissions, compared to 36 percent of hospitals serving wealthier populations.[1] While researchers and medical professionals recognize that lower-income patients have limited resources for health maintenance, the penalties remain the same. Decreased Medicare reimbursement directly contributed to the closure of twenty-one US hospitals in 2016, including St Joseph's hospital in North Philadelphia, a 135-bed facility that served one of the poorest sections of the city.[2]

Even if someone is eligible for coverage, Medicare isn't free. If recipients earn less than $85,000 a year, their monthly premiums are $134. Add this to the 20 percent co-pay for services, plus out-of-pocket costs for medications. With certain Medicare Part D prescription plans, Medicare will not pay for prescriptions until a $400 deductible is met. Once the plan has paid $3,700 for medications, individuals' payments increase.

As with most fees in our capitalist health care system, costs are only rising annually.[3] Bernie Sanders' ninety-six-page Medicare for All bill (S. 1804) is purposefully vague. He asserts that patients will have no co-pays, premiums or deductibles, yet gives no details of what will be paid for. He speaks of a formulary of medications to be covered by the program, but no mention of restrictions on what pharmaceutical companies can charge, and no limits on lobbying by drug companies. It is no surprise that Sanders' bill is supported by recipients of pharmaceutical company donations like Democratic New Jersey Senator Cory Booker. Even if it would become law, eighteen to thirty-five-year-olds would start receiving coverage four years after universal Medicare is implemented, much too late for people who need help right now.

Yet Sanders said that he does not expect this bill to pass. The proposal he is making to adequately

> **"WHY DO WE SEEK OUT A GOVERN-MENT-BASED SOLUTION WHEN MEDICARE HAS ALREADY FAILED SO MANY?"**

and completely cover all Americans is not allowed under our current political system. There is too much at stake. Private insurance companies, drug manufacturers, medical equipment suppliers, and those receiving money from these groups do not want the system to change. It's simply too profitable. If lawmakers cannot accept an increase in Medicare and Medicaid coverage, there is no chance for a radical change through legislative channels.

REVOLUTION, NOT REFORMS

Reforms are never permanent and are never an end goal. As we saw with attempts to dismantle the Affordable Care Act (ACA), any move toward helping the general population can be reversed at the whims of those in power. The United States imagines itself a democracy but nothing could be farther from the truth. Those in power are not concerned with the popularity of programs and reforms, and instead serve only their own interests. Only 25 to 35 percent of voters supported President Trump's GOP tax reform bill, yet senators and representatives pushed it through because it serves the needs of the wealthy. They are listening to their benefactors and not their constituents. The state does not have the interests of the working class in mind and never has, yet progressives continue to look to government to provide basic needs.

The state has never been in favor of affordable medical treatment. Historically, US leaders pushed against universal health care in favor of employer-sponsored insurance. In 1942, President Franklin D. Roosevelt imposed a freeze on wages called the Stabilization Act. In response, unions acted to advocate for workers. They started negotiating benefits and pensions, including health insurance, in order to provide laborers with something to replace lost income. At that time, private insurance was part of the employee benefit package and did not include co-pays and premiums.

Six years later, in 1949, President Harry S. Truman's proposal of universal health care was met with fears that it would lead the country to communism. What happened was that health insurance was turned into a profit-heavy capitalist system. Almost seventy years after Truman rejected universal coverage, the highest salary for a health insurance CEO is $22 million a year.[4]

It makes sense that people want to stop inflated health care costs and obscene salaries, but reforms do nothing to change the core systems. When President Obama enacted the ACA in 2010, it did not reduce the power insurance companies have over consumers. The government required companies to take on enrollees who spent the most on health care—the elderly, chronically ill, and people with preexisting conditions. They did, but passed on that cost by raising premiums. In turn, people who could not afford the monthly costs were back to being uninsured or struggling to pay.

The largest benefit gained from the ACA was the expansion of Medicaid. Over sixteen million people became covered for the first time, allowing them access to preventative and routine health care as well as mental health and substance abuse treatment. In Pennsylvania, over 124,000 people struggling with drug and alcohol addiction entered Medicaid-paid detox and rehabilitation for the first time. Enter Paul Ryan, who, after the approval of the GOP tax bill, said that Medicaid and Medicare were "entitlement programs" and announced the Republicans' plan to cut spending on both programs in 2018.

> "IF LAWMAKERS CANNOT ACCEPT AN INCREASE IN MEDICARE AND MEDICAID COVERAGE, THERE IS NO CHANCE FOR A RADICAL CHANGE THROUGH LEGISLATIVE CHANNELS."

This is the natural progression for a government that has already cut funding to the Children's Health Insurance Program (CHIP), which provides healthcare to millions of children with parents who are low-income but do not qualify for Medicaid. Both Democrats and Republicans showed that they do not need popular support to pass bills and cut programs. They simply decide what poor people deserve.

ANOTHER HEALTH CARE SYSTEM IS POSSIBLE

As people begin to realize that the health care, pharmaceutical, and private and government industries are not serving them, groups are working independently without the support or resources of the state to give care where it is needed. For them, there is no lobbying for the next health care plan or waiting for bills to pass. There is just direct action and building dual power—the concept that communities are served by and responsible to themselves. There is no hierarchy and no reliance on the state for grants and oversight.

As with many dual power organizations, we see more forming outside of the US Some, like the Self-Organized Health Structure of Exarchia (ADYE) in Greece, were born out of the economic crisis and growing illegitimacy of the government. Within the largely leftist Athens neighborhood of Exarchia, a community grew as an anarchist hub for those who wished to resist oppression by police, and increasingly from fascist groups.

The ADYE operates solely through volunteer caregivers and donations of money and supplies. Staffed by physicians, radiologists, therapists, dentists and nurses among others, ADYE serves anyone in need. The goal is a completely self-run, egalitarian health service to provide basic care to those who need it, regardless of ability to pay. They refer more complicated cases to local hospitals, but the ASYE provides care for general ailments and preventative healthcare.

In the US, Hurricanes Katrina and Harvey sparked health care mutual aid out of necessity and the desire to help when the government and NGOs were not meeting needs. Common Ground Relief, an anarchist collective touting the motto "Solidarity not Charity," started in a mosque and on the streets of New Orleans in the aftermath of Hurricane Katrina. Following the closure of Charity Hospital, Common Ground's clinic provided traditional and alternative health care to over sixty thousand people.

Similarly, medics with Bayou Action Street Health (BASH) took to the streets of Houston after the hurricane, reaching people who were still waiting for NGO relief. They transported residents for medical care and staged pop-up clinics throughout the city. Several mutual aid groups continue their disaster relief work through loose networks in Puerto Rico, Mexico, California, and Texas. They are often the only groups who show up to help in poor and underserved areas. After the emergency work is finished, mutual aid groups are staying in the communities to provide health care, long after the Red Cross and other relief groups have left. Recipients of mutual aid and street medic care often say that they build trust through their on-the-ground presence and nonjudgment.

Judgment and scapegoating are also factors in the lack of affordable care for substance abuse. Last October, after years of increased opioid addiction and overdose, Donald Trump declared the national opioid crisis a "Health Emergency;" but instead of providing funding for care, he placed blame on addicts while offering hollow gestures akin to the grossly ineffective "Just Say No" campaign of the 1980s. To fill in gaps left by the government and other nonprofits, Prevention Point in Philadelphia has been on the front lines of harm reduction for twenty-five years, providing syringe exchange, HIV testing and counseling, wound care, legal services, overdose reversal training, and detox and rehabilitation referrals.

The Mayor and Board of Health authorized their efforts, and they negotiated agreements with local law enforcement to prevent the arrest of heroin users. Their work, provided free of charge, is invaluable. A recent report showed that out of the high-risk groups susceptible to HIV infection, the IV drug using population was the only group to have a drop in infection rates, from 23 percent in 2004 to 10 percent in 2010. Newly elected Philadelphia District Attorney and civil rights lawyer Larry Krasner said he is in support of safe injection sites in the city, which Prevention Point has advocated for.

Resources and funding are always an issue when providing care outside of the traditional health care system. Organizations can accept donations like food, water, bandages and scanning equipment without restriction, but medications and needles are closely regulated by the FDA and local law enforcement. Safety-net pharmacies are filling the need for free medications unencumbered by insurance company formularies and co-pays. Clinics receive donated, unexpired medicines, and they then match available medications to patients in need. Prescriptions are required, but there are no insurance authorizations and no money changes hands. Free clinics and Direct Patient Care, a throwback to old style physician-patient relationships, also aim to treat patients without involving insurance.

BUILDING A SYSTEM: NEXT STEPS

Health care without the state and corporate insurance can happen, but implementation necessitates small steps. It requires evidence of success to take away the fear of abandoning a system of health care delivery that's been in place for over seventy years. As people realize they can receive quality and affordable health care without worrying about swinging pendulums of reform, and without the undue influence and persistent failures of federal and private insurance companies, the state loses legitimacy and the working class gains power.

We first need the resources to build systems that work. As natural disasters inevitably increase, there will be an ongoing need for relief workers at the ready to provide care. We require an increase in trained and licensed leftist physicians, nurses, pharmacists, paramedics, mental health professionals, and alternative medicine practitioners so this direct work can continue beyond disaster relief and gain credibility. As more anarchists enter the health care field, they will be able to shape institutional policies, organize workers to demand better patient care and working conditions, and build and adequately staff new mutual aid programs.

Current anarchist health care workers can encourage an increase in radical professionals by mentoring and teaching students and those interested in medical work. Those with training can provide street medic training and free first aid classes for underserved communities. There is also a need for a revolutionary faction in current unions and creation of new, nonhierarchical patient and worker unions.

Secondly, we need money to pay for services and supplies. This is unfortunately an all too common reality in the capitalist system. As health care services for the working class are increasingly underfunded or eliminated, we can no longer assume that Medicaid and Medicare will always be available. The push for privatization will likely cause for-profit health insurance companies to become the only option for most Americans. However, people can give funds directly for care instead of to insurance companies who siphon it directly into their profits.

Here in Lancaster County, Pennsylvania, the Amish practice a "from each according to ability and to each according to need" approach to medical payments. While they are a religious order and not Marxist, they are collectivist and care for each other. Individuals and families contribute to a liability insurance fund based on assets and income. This fund, combined with contributions from the church, proceeds from fundraisers, and discounts negotiated with local providers, pays for the entirety of community members' hospital bills.

In other areas of the country, five states offer health insurance cooperatives using the same mutual aid strategies. Co-ops suffered a blow under the Obama administration when the federal government withheld previously promised funding for smaller insurance companies, including co-ops, under the Risk Corridor Program. In other cases of "too big to fail," the government issued subsidies to larger companies to keep them afloat. The Trump administration has also threatened to cut funding for health insurance co-ops. Government subsidies pump millions of dollars into insurance companies that in turn funnel millions to candidates in exchange for favorable legislation and policies. For-profit insurance will never work to benefit the consumer; therefore the best response is nonparticipation.

Lastly, and perhaps most importantly, is our need to build anarchist networks to create a viable health care system. Any alternative to the current health care system is going to start slowly and locally. One clinic in Philadelphia may inspire another in Pittsburgh. They share ideas on what works with interested anarchists in Cleveland, who then talk with an anarchist nurse they know in San Francisco. This is how revolutionary change happens.

As a primary goal, Medicare for All is reformist and not revolutionary. Universal health care is a temporary solution under the current capitalist health care system, but anarchists can reach for a genuinely socialized system based on self-management and cooperation. We know what kind of health care services our communities need. When we have doctors, nurses and other practitioners working together in a decentralized environment, providing care directly to patients without worry of insurance co-pays, this is where we build power. And no one can take that away.

FOR FURTHER READING

Self-Organized Health Structure of Exarchia (ADYE): https://en.squat.net/tag/k-vox/

Bayou Action Street Health (BASH): https://www.facebook.com/BayouActionStreetHealth/

Common Ground Relief: scott crow, *Black Flags and Windmills: Hope, Anarchy, and the Common Ground Collective* (Oakland, CA: PM Press, 2014).

Prevention Point Philadelphia: https://ppponline.org

ABOUT THE AUTHOR

Sarah Miller is currently in her fifth year as an RN, having spent the prior ten years as a mental health professional. She is involved with Red Rose Socialists in Lancaster, PA and is an integrating member of Black Rose/Rosa Negra Anarchist Federation in Philadelphia, PA.

ENDNOTES

1. J. Rau, "Medicare fines 2,610 hospitals in third round of readmission penalties." *The Inquirer*, October 3, 2014. Available at http://www.philly.com/philly/health/healthcare-exchange/Medicare_fines_2610_hospitals_in_third_round_of_readmission_penalties.html.

2. J. George, "St. Joseph's Hospital closing tied to reduction in state financial support." *Philadelphia Business Journal*, December 30, 2015.

3. Medicare.gov, "Costs at a glance." 2018. Available at https://www.medicare.gov/your-medicare-costs/costs-at-a-glance/costs-at-glance.html.

4. R. Siegel, and C. Columbus, "As Cost Of US Health Care Skyrockets, So Does Pay Of Health Care CEOs." National Public Radio, July 26, 2017. Available at:
https://www.npr.org/sections/health-shots/2017/07/26/539518682/
as-cost-of-u-s-health-care-skyrockets-so-does-pay-of-health-care-ceos.

Art by Josh MacPhee | Justseeds.org

THE COOPERATIVE COMMONWEALTH: AN ANARCHISM FOR THE 21ST CENTURY?

ROBERT CHRISTL

« Art by Roger Peet | Justseeds.org

MUTUAL AID ASSOCIATIONS have historically emerged from disenfranchised populations' struggle to survive inequality. During the late nineteenth century, when European and American states offered little social welfare, the destitute pragmatically combined their resources out of necessity. Meanwhile, anarchists recognized that workers' mutual aid associations, such as benefit societies, labor unions, and cooperatives pointed to an alternate world, and they actively participated in them with the intention of fostering a new society.[1] Such a perspective is a hallmark of Left libertarian thought, and its relevance today is paramount as pro-austerity governments dismantle the liberal welfare state.

Geographer and anarchist Pyotr Kropotkin presented various species' cooperative sociability as a "natural law" in a series of articles which he republished as *Mutual Aid: A Factor of Evolution* (1902). Tracing mutual aid's evolution from the ant colony to the medieval guild, Kropotkin claimed that animals and humans instinctively band together to survive harsh environments. The Spanish revolutionary Diego Abad de Santillán made a similar observation in 1936 when he declared that the "soviets were a fact before they were a theory."[2] Modern anarchism, he argued, needed to cultivate laborers' tendency towards a sociable existence through contemporary working-class institutions such as labor unions. Today, Andrej Grubačić and Denis O'Hearn posit the practices and spaces of Cossacks, Zapatistas, and prisoners in the American justice system as local resistances to global capitalism.[3] The state, acting as capitalism's midwife, pushed such groups to the geographic or social edges of society, forcing them to imagine a different and better world along the lines of mutual aid. These analyses remind us that organizations designed to resist inequality can also prefigure its overcoming. One of the revolutionary's duties is to assist mutual aid organizations in universalizing their more egalitarian logic to overcome hierarchies.

This essay encourages radical democrats, who are equally concerned with achieving social justice and realizing it by open and horizontal means, to take an active role in the emerging alliance between municipal governments and cooperatives in the United States. Madison, Wisconsin serves as an example in which the city and an array of social movements have coalesced to cultivate a worker-owned cooperative economy in opposition to the economic and racial inequalities aggravated by capitalism and government policies. The aim is to analyze this coalition in its historical context, highlight its potential, and illustrate how radical democrats' involvement can help steer capitalism and the state toward the Cooperative Commonwealth: a federated, socialist, and participatory society.

SYSTEMIC CHANGE AND ITS CONDITIONS OF POSSIBILITY

The Great Recession serves as a backdrop to the political crises of the last decade and the growing cooperative movement. While a straight line cannot be drawn from today's issues to Lehman Brothers' filing bankruptcy, the economic downturn aggravated preexisting inequalities and disillusionment with American democracy, contributing to a general sense of cynicism regarding the order of things. In the United States, the economic turmoil of recent years has contributed to a deeper crisis of representative government. Frustration with professional politicians and their managerial politics, which neutralize democracy and preserve the status quo, erupted following the Obama years, resulting in Bernie Sanders' newfound popularity and Donald Trump's presidential victory.[4] Markets' recovery has not produced an improvement in workers' conditions and wages. Moreover, mass incarceration continues to destroy Black communities, while law enforcement's harassment of poor Black and Latino neighborhoods worsens living conditions.

In other words, many people for many different reasons feel that they have been cheated by the system and that government by, for, and of the people is a façade. And yet despite widespread disillusionment in America, the political parameters of neoliberalism have not yet broken.[5] It is within these circumstances that the idea of the Cooperative Commonwealth has slowly begun to take hold, especially in city politics.

Since the recession, and especially after Trump's inauguration, cities have emerged as a crucial site of progressive policies and resistance. Given Republican control of the federal government and most state governments, some cities have used what autonomy they possess to ameliorate the systemic changes that lowered Americans' quality of life. In the last few years, municipal governments have declared their cities sanctuaries for immigrants, pledged to adhere to the Paris Climate Accord, and raised the minimum wage. Nevertheless, such reforms do not imply the prefigurative politics needed to imagine, build, and cement a different world.

From the outset, twenty-first century radical democrats face three obstacles that limit our efforts to steer economic and political changes towards more just societies, making municipal cooperativism the most realistic and radical path forward. Foremost, whereas the turn of the twentieth-century Left beamed with optimism about the end of capitalism and the disappearance of the state, today's Left suffers from a profound crisis of uncertainty about what comes next. If the early twentieth century promised redemptive catastrophe, today we are faced with ecological catastrophe if we continue along the same route of economic development. Yet leaping into the abyss inspires no confidence if there is no promise of landing on socialism.

Secondly, despite the disintegration of states in places like Chiapas and Rojava, the proliferation of public-private enterprises in social services, schooling, and utilities, and the existence of transnational institutions like the European Union, the nation-state as a governing entity and object of mass identification is not going anywhere soon. Unlike the period stretching from the 1860s to the First World War, characterized by consolidating and vulnerable nation-states in places such as the United States, Italy, Spain, Russia, Japan, and Argentina (where anarchists attracted mass support), today there is no corresponding widespread re-imagination of territorial sovereignty and its mechanisms.[6] Global capitalism is altering rather than drastically reducing the power of states and their apparatuses. Capital's institutions—the IMF, World Bank, and European Union, to name some—are built on nation-states and impose capital's demands through them.

Relatedly, American society is marked by the entrenchment of statist officialdom. The official web of decision-making bodies, bureaucratic apparatuses, laws, regulations, and public institutions, naturalized by Americans' civic and popular cultures, remains resistant against radical change. Moreover, reformist efforts over the course of the twentieth century to push officialdom towards progressive economic policies have been repeatedly defeated since the 1970s, and civil society's ability to influence or intervene in officialdom has been drastically reduced. Unionization, for example, is down to pre-Depression levels. Third parties remain marginal. Republicans and Democrats continue to possess a monopoly on power at the federal and state level, enabling them to reduce the terms of political debate. What is more, officialdom frustrates efforts to articulate radical solutions to perennial problems such as inequality. Despite widespread recognition that something is fundamentally wrong with our Republic, the state itself is not subject to criticism. In short: there is no shared stateless imaginary today.

Yet the relative loss of faith in capitalism (which is widely perceived as decoupled from statist officialdom; so-called bad government is identified as the problem, not the state form itself) and frustration with the quality of representative politics in America offers space for a critical move in the long struggle against contemporary capitalism and its state. The question at hand is at which site do we concentrate popular aspirations? Where do we build our new world? The municipal-cooperative alliance is one promising site of struggle.

INCUBATING THE COOPERATIVE COMMONWEALTH IN WISCONSIN

Although they make up a relatively small portion of the state's economy today, co-ops have a long history in Wisconsin. According to a 2012 study conducted by the University of Wisconsin-Madison Center for Cooperatives, there are around 770 active cooperatives in the state, with agriculture leading and credit unions and retail stores in second and third place. As a whole, Wisconsin's co-ops generate around $17.2 billion in annual sales, $1.5 billion in wages, and 35,000 jobs.[7]

Recently, there has been a noticeable growth in interest in Madison, Wisconsin's capital, regarding co-ops. The city's municipal-cooperative alliance is part of a growing national trend. From New York to California, city governments and social movements are pursuing alternate forms of economic organization. Co-op incubators such as the Cincinnati Union Co-op Initiative (CUCI), Cooperation Jackson, and the Madison Cooperative Development Coalition (MCDC) have emerged to coordinate efforts between city politicians and activists in funding co-ops and training worker-owners. The combined impact of the Great Recession and neoliberals' top-down austerity, as well as longer and more local histories of poverty and institutional racism, have invigorated interest in cooperative economies as a way of empowering marginalized communities.

The turn to co-ops in Madison has short-term and long-term roots. In many ways, Wisconsin's recent history epitomizes the systemic shift from industrial production to a technology- and service-based economy in parts of the global north. For example, decades before the Great Recession, workers in south-central Wisconsin were already feeling the strains of a sluggish economy, due in part to gradual deindustrialization, the collapse of local businesses reliant on heavy industry, and the transition towards a service sector economy without the same labor protections and living standards previously won by unions' historic struggles.[8] The recession exacerbated this situation, contributing to the popular discontent on which governor Scott Walker's electoral victory capitalized in 2010.

Walker's campaign channeled existing feelings of resentment and uncertainty among rural populations who felt that Wisconsin's major cities—Madison and Milwaukee—absorbed more than their fair share of the state's wealth. Walker's campaigns spoke to the economic hardship of rural communities and their animosity towards the supposedly undeserving cities. He mobilized rural constituencies that had relied on disappearing heavy industry and the economies which supplied it. Like Trump, Walker strategically misdiagnosed the causes of workers' misery. He took aim at liberal white-collar Madison and its public sector employees and their unions, blaming the capital's government-based economy and the University of Wisconsin-Madison for the rest of the state's woes.[9]

Following the neoliberal formula of using crises as a pretext for savage cuts and deregulation, Walker and the Republican-dominated Senate and state Assembly stripped unions of their collective bargaining rights with the infamous Act 10, passed in early 2011. They have since slashed the state budget, deregulated environmental protections, and centralized power in the governorship. To cement his status as one of the most aggressive neoliberals, Walker sealed a deal with Foxconn in 2017. The electronics manufacturer (which has overworked Chinese employees to the point of suicide) promised to build a massive plant in Wisconsin in exchange for three billion dollars in government subsidies.[10]

The economic devastation caused by Republicans in recent years has aggravated inequalities with a longer history in Wisconsin, making the state one of the worst places to live for individuals and families of color. Reports indicate that the level of economic disparity between

> "IF THE EARLY TWENTIETH CENTURY PROMISED REDEMPTIVE CATASTROPHE, TODAY WE ARE FACED WITH ECOLOGICAL CATASTROPHE IF WE CONTINUE ALONG THE SAME ROUTE OF ECONOMIC DEVELOPMENT."

Black and white Americans in Wisconsin remains one of the widest in the country. On average, unemployment in the Black community is three times higher than among whites. Moreover, many Black families' median household income is half of what it is in white households.[11] One of the most visible issues has been the regular evictions which keep some Black families at perpetual risk of homelessness.[12] Forced out of middle-class, student, and yuppie neighborhoods, many Black residents have been pushed towards the margins, away from essential services as well as social and civic life.

These are the conditions in which talks between Madison's Mayor Paul Soglin, President of the South-Central Federation of Labor Kevin Gundlach, and then Director of the University of Wisconsin's Center for Cooperatives Anne Reynolds began to crystallize around the idea of the city making resources available for new co-ops. In 2016 the city's Department of Planning and Community Economic Development put out a request for proposals and began meeting with the MCDC. The Coalition, comprised of local labor unions, immigrant and racial justice organizations, and developers dedicated to promoting cooperatives, came together in early 2016. The MCDC's immediate goal was to write a grant proposal asking the city to provide the financial resources to grow Madison's cooperative economy among marginalized and impoverished communities. From the beginning, labor, racial justice, and community activists approached the grant writing process collaboratively rather than competing with each other over scarce resources. In the long term, the MCDC aims to train community-based organizations to offer the education and resources needed to their own constituencies. This will make co-op development an integral part of their mission to empower communities through good jobs, self-determination, and a broader communitarian culture.

The city and the MCDC signed the final contract in January 2017. Three million dollars, to be spent over five years, would be invested in the creation of worker-owned cooperatives in Madison. The funding would go towards technical assistance and low-interest loans to support unionized worker-owned co-ops.

In allocating these resources, Madisonians adopted an ecosystemic approach in which multiple actors, such as the city government and the social movements that constitute the MCDC, coordinate the distribution of resources with the explicit purpose of creating a self-sustaining economy of mutual aid among impoverished communities.[13] Early on, the players involved recognized that transformative social change needs more than just government money indiscriminately given to whomever applies. Cultivating an economy along the lines of mutual aid requires broad-based and coordinated participation by Madison's different communities as well as a concerted effort by activists to forge those connections. Rather than simply making loans available, privileging existing cooperatives with city contracts, or inserting co-ops within public sector supply chains to guarantee them a market, the city government empowered the MCDC to oversee the three million dollars' investment in a new cooperative bedrock. In other words, Madisonians' efforts to grow the cooperative economy is led by the grassroots. While the city provides crucial elements such as financing, business connections, and advocacy, the social movements channel these resources to those communities that need them most.

> "DESPITE THE POSITIVE RESULTS THUS FAR, THE COOPERATIVE MOVEMENT FACES OBSTACLES THAT THREATEN ITS GAINS AND OBFUSCATE ITS RADICAL POLITICS."

When I spoke with Reynolds, she said progress on the project has been made, albeit slowly. Although the MCDC's steering committee meets every two weeks, the discussions still focus on how best to implement this complex project. "It's ambitious, this level of decentralization," said Reynolds. She noted that the MCDC is composed of twenty-eight different organizations, but not everyone has a common understanding of what a co-op is or what it should accomplish. This poses a serious challenge. "We have never envisioned a one-size-fits-all set of workshops on co-ops." Reynolds pointed out for example the need to tailor co-ops to the Latino community's specific needs in terms of goods and services.[14]

Reynolds is realistic about the potential of the municipal-cooperative alliance to bring about the Cooperative Commonwealth anytime soon. Today, much of the interest in cooperatives is utilitarian. It seems like a good way of doing business, but there is little appreciation of the radical democratic seed dormant in the worker-owned and worker-managed enterprises. For example, she noted that there are vast differences between what co-op supporters in Madison and Milwaukee envision compared to those from the rest of the state. So far, much of the interest in co-ops has come from entrepreneurs steeped in an individualist model of business start-ups. A great deal of work needs to be done to create a community-wide understanding about what the co-op is and should be, and the politics latent in its worker-owned model. According to Reynolds, the plan for 2018 is to increase co-ops' visibility through public and community-specific forums. Beyond convincing consumers to patronize co-ops, the movement aims to cultivate an explicitly communitarian culture that replaces the egoism of typical capitalist enterprises. In this sense, Reynolds admitted that the MCDC is far behind Cooperation Jackson, the Mississippi movement dedicated to creating a network of co-ops among the impoverished Black and Latino working class. Nevertheless, at a joint symposium held by the MCDC and CUCI in Madison on February 7, 2018, MCDC announced the incorporation of its first unionized worker-owned co-op, the accounting firm Common Good Bookkeeping.

ACTUALIZING THE COOPERATIVE COMMONWEALTH

Despite the positive results thus far, the cooperative movement faces obstacles that threaten its gains and obfuscate its radical politics. Most obviously, the initial reliance on the state places the movement at the mercy of friendly city councils and mayors. While progressives can be convinced to set aside a modest amount of resources for co-ops, business-friendly liberals pose as much a threat as Republicans to their funding and advocacy. In Madison's case, the city made it clear at the beginning of the budget process that it did not intend to make a recurring investment in co-ops. The community-based organizations were told to develop alternate sustainability models. However, it is difficult to accumulate enough capital to launch new co-ops since the MCDC is working with low-income people. Few institutions like the municipality (or the labor unions, which have been crucial to the Madisonian movement) can offer the resources needed to fund and train new cooperatives.

Secondly, worker cooperatives are not inherently egalitarian beyond the principle of one member, one vote. Internal hierarchies may take shape through wage differentials between staff and elected managers. Temporary or seasonal employees can be subjected to secondary status as non-members, which can impact their decision-making power on the basis that they are somehow less invested in the co-op's success. Moreover, worker-owned businesses are still capable of reproducing a complacency towards the general economic order once workers have acquired "their fair share" of a corrupt system.

Lastly, it is easier to convert an existing business into a worker-owned cooperative than to build one from scratch. However, cooperativization of a traditional capitalist enterprise requires that the owner or owners' consent to selling the business or some of its assets to employees. Despite the fact that both capital and labor are needed to launch an enterprise, private property laws arbitrarily treat the capitalist as the venture's owner, with complete control over the business's existence. While some capitalists are happy to pass along their business to employees eventually, they are not obligated to hand it over. Madison's budget allocation for co-ops offers funding to train workers on how to convert an existing business into a cooperative. Nevertheless, the boss's initial 'ownership' and ultimate decision-making power over the business remains unaltered.

So, what is to be done? The nation-state continues to be entrenched in our daily lives and still defends capitalists' interests. What is more, communicating to a popular audience what comes after the modern nation-state and capitalism is difficult and perhaps even counterproductive. Writing in 1938, after the anarcho-syndicalist move-ment collaborated with the Republican government during the Spanish Civil War against General Franco, Joan Peiró, one of the movement's leaders, struggled to adapt anarchist thought to the new reality of the near-indestructible liberal democratic state. He wrote: "For almost a century, anarchism has fought the state from outside. And yet, instead of shrinking, every day the state's authority and power grows."[15] Anarchists like Peiró who collaborated with the Republic during the war hoped to restrain it and devolve its functions, giving the collectives which emerged during the simultaneous Spanish Revolution a chance to develop. Replacing the state's authoritarian struc-tures with committees accountable to the unions, legalizing worker expropriations, funneling state resources to collectivized enterprises, improving working conditions, and providing social services represented an attempt by Spanish anarchists to adapt anarchism's radical democratic politics to overwhelming historical conditions. It is a lesson worth keeping in mind today when faced with the ability of the state and capitalism to crush almost any effort to cultivate societies outside their grasp.

The capacity of municipal cooperativism to lay the groundwork for the Cooperative Commonwealth requires radical democrats to invest their energies in municipal government. Or, to borrow from Murray Bookchin, the goal is to produce a "clear and uncompromising" tension between people's municipalities and domi-neering federal and state governments.[16] By pressuring individuals running for office to commit to funding worker-owned co-ops among marginalized populations, or better yet devolving the local state apparatus and economy to ourselves through direct intervention in municipal governance, we can hasten this tension and gradually—hopefully—displace capitalism. Our aim should be to intervene in local governance to reinvent how decision-making occurs and redirect where state resources go.

City government's greater proximity to the people than state or federal govern-ments offers potentially a more direct relationship between representatives and repre-sented until a more participatory form of self-governance can be institutionalized. *At the very least*, we can collectively occupy and lobby at council meetings. *Ideally*, radical democrats can introduce a new political culture and cooperative agenda themselves by winning seats. During the Wisconsin Uprising and Occupy Wall Street, protestors set up assemblies in which open discussion and horizontal decision-making, as well as an ethos of solidarity, prefigured the kinds of practices we hope to universalize. Yet such assemblies proved ephemeral. What would the introduction and institutionalization of such practices into state bodies like the municipal council look like? How might such "popular" councils collaborate with and coordinate a growing cooperative economy?

Our ability to democratize municipal governance and cooperativize local econ-omies depends largely on seizing the city council itself. As Madison shows, alliances with progressives can only go so far. Investment in a cooperative economy cannot be a onetime thing. It requires the funding and coordinating capacity the city can offer, but the only way of securing such resources is by electing radical democrats to city office. Moreover, there are important strategic considerations. Elections for city councils are often nonpartisan, opening space for candidates outside of the two parties. Also, a lower number of voters in municipal elections means that organized support for a radical democratic candidate has a decent chance of success. Lastly, municipal government is an opportunity to put in practice the old slogan popularized by anarchists that "any cook can govern." Rotating representatives between terms can preserve an interventionist relationship with officialdom while affirming our connection with the social movements.

Of course, such an approach to officialdom should be complemented by an investment of activists' energies in the cultural work of diffusing a cooperative worldview within civil society. This calls for the translation of radical democratic ideas into Americans' civic vernacular. Despite the excitement surrounding Bernie Sanders' presidential campaign, most Americans will never read Kropotkin or wave the red flag. We should acknowledge this and instead work towards reinscribing the quotidian with a radical meaning to produce a new common sense regarding the purpose and potential of politics. The widespread acceptance of the category of "the 99%," and its reorientation of the political field, is the best example in recent memory. Radical democrats must infiltrate governments, businesses, unions, community organizations, and co-ops to convince people at all levels of society to support the cooperative economy in terms they recognize.

This requires extensive researching and organizing beforehand. Madison's cooperative project is fortunate in that the labor movement and racial justice organizations are already heavily involved. Radical democrats need to make strategic decisions that account for the budget-writing process, friendly city councillors and mayors (or winnable seats), and local social movements with whom to coordinate. This is not glamorous work, but it offers the most realistic path forward in this moment.

CONCLUSION

Over a century ago, anarchists, communists, and social democrats also attempted to pinpoint the site from which revolution would unfold. After the specter of the Paris Commune seemed exorcised, the European bourgeoisie eased its repression of socialist movements during the 1890s. Such an opening of limited political space witnessed an explosion in working-class organizational and intellectual activity. The waves of turn-of-the-century strikes, from Spain in 1902 to Russia in 1905, led thinkers such as Anselmo Lorenzo and Rosa Luxemburg to see in the strike a valuable tool in the revolutionary process. Two decades later, after the Russian Revolution and Italy's Red Biennium, worker councils' direct expropriation of factories and fields became another site of revolutionary possibility alongside the general strike. Today, the same kind of strategic recognition is required. Municipal cooperativism is a product of contemporary capitalism's crises. It has emerged at the intersection of the historical processes outlined here, and it represents a rich site at which the popular classes can coalesce. In other words, history has determined the field of struggle. Our task is to ensure the institutionalization of the municipal cooperative through political and cultural work.

ABOUT THE AUTHOR

Robert Christl is a graduate student at the University of Wisconsin-Madison working on the history of anarchism in Spain. He is an active member of the Teaching Assistants Association and a delegate to Wisconsin's South-Central Federation of Labor.

ENDNOTES

1. Errico Malatesta was an important advocate of anarchist participation in workers' associations, even if they did not adhere to anarchist principles. In his discussion of the bakers' union founded in 1887 in Buenos Aires, in which Malatesta and other anarchists played an important role, Gonzalo Zaragoza claims: "Anarchist or revolutionary ideologies did not explicitly appear… However, the presence of anarchist militants in the society's steering committee marked its ideological line." Gonzalo Zaragoza, *Anarquismo Argentino* (1876-1902) (Madrid: De la Torre, 1996), 97.
2. Diego Abad de Santillán, El organismo económico de la revolución (Bilbao: Zero, 1978), 62.
3. Andrej Grubačić and Denis O'Hearn, *Living at the Edges of Capitalism: Adventures in Exile and Mutual Aid* (Berkeley: University of California Press, 2016), 6.
4. In both 2008 and 2012, Barack Obama won Wisconsin. During the 2016 presidential primaries, Bernie Sanders soundly defeated Hillary Clinton by 13.54 percentage points, capturing the rural vote; meanwhile Donald Trump lost to Ted Cruz. In the presidential elections, rural districts that had gone to Obama and Sanders flipped for Trump, giving him the state's delegates.
5. Wendy Brown, *Undoing the Demos: Neoliberalism's Stealth Revolution* (Cambridge: MIT Press, 2015).
6. See Sho Konishi, *Anarchist Modernity: Cooperatism and Japanese-Russian Intellectual Relations in Modern Japan* (Cambridge: Harvard University Asia Center, 2013) and Guillermo Palacios and Erika Pani, El poder y la sangre: guerra, estado y nación en la década de 1860 (Ciudad de México: Colegio de México, 2014).
7. Lynn Pitman, "Economic Impacts of Cooperative Firms in Wisconsin: an Overview." (University of Wisconsin-Madison Center for Cooperatives, 2014), 3. Available at http://www.uwcc.wisc.edu/pdf/WI%20Impacts%20summary_2014.pdf.
8. Camille Kerr, "Local Government Support for Cooperatives," Austin Co-op Summit 2015, Democracy at Work Institute, 2. Available at http://www.uwcc.wisc.edu/pdf/local%20govt%20support.pdf.
9. Katherine J. Cramer, *The Politics of Resentment: Rural Consciousness in Wisconsin and the Rise of Scott Walker* (Chicago: University of Chicago Press, 2016).
10. Brian Merchant, "Life and Death in Apple's Forbidden City." *The Guardian*, June 18, 2017, available at https://www.theguardian.com/technology/2017/jun/18/foxconn-life-death-forbidden-city-longhua-suicide-apple-iphone-brian-merchant-one-device-extract.
11. J. Carlisle Larsen, "Wisconsin Considered One Of The Worst states For Racial Disparities", *Wisconsin Public Radio*, January 19, 2017, available at https://www.wpr.org/wisconsin-considered-one-worst-states-racial-disparities.

12. Matthew Desmond, *Evicted: Poverty and Profit in the American City* (New York: Broadway Books, 2017).

13. Michelle Camou, "Cities Developing Worker Co-ops: Efforts in Ten Cities." *Imagined Economy Project,* August 8, 2016, available at http://imaginedeconomy.org/wp-content/up-loads/2016/08/report3_citycoops.pdf.

14. Anne Reynolds, "Madison's Cooperative Economy," interview by Robert Christl, January 4, 2018.

15. Joan Peiró, "El estado, el anarquismo y la historía," in Timón, 1938.

16. Murray Bookchin, *The Murray Bookchin Reader*, ed. Janet Biehl (London and Washington: Cassell, 1997), 179.

SIGNS OF THE REVOLUTION: DEAF JUSTICE AND ANARCHIST PRAXIS

TRISTAN WRIGHT

THE DEAF COMMUNITY IS A SO-ciolinguistic minority in the United States. While most people are familiar with terms like "racism," "sexism," "white supremacy," or "patriarchy," they are unlikely to have heard the word used to describe oppression of d/Deaf people: "audism." The oppression faced by d/Deaf and hard of hearing people in the larger hearing society is often totally overlooked or even perpetuated not only by the average hearing person, but by those in anarchist and social justice circles. When is the last time you saw an interpreter at a rally? When's the last time the rally had a Deaf speaker? When thinking about an issue like police brutality, how many activists include the experiences of d/Deaf and hard of hearing people alongside our critiques of law enforcement?

A broader understanding of oppression is necessary if we are interested in creating a truly just and equitable world. A major aspect of accessibility for d/Deaf and hard of hearing people is the work of interpreters. Anarchists interested in combatting oppression on all its fronts will need to make connections with Deaf activists and organizers, and to challenge our own assumptions and biases about language, access, and communication. Some of that effort will involve connecting with interpreters, and some will involve learning new ways of interacting. In the end, it may demand of hearing anarchists that we re-envision our revolutionary activity to be not only inclusive, but equitable. After all, what revolution is it if not everyone can participate?

LANGUAGE, AUDIOLOGY AND POLITICS

For more than a century, use of American Sign Language, or ASL, has been suppressed by hearing people who have argued that Deaf individuals must use spoken and written English—in other words, to act as if they are hearing—to survive in society at large. Yet Deaf people throughout the years have continued to use their native language and share it with d/Deaf, hard of hearing, and hearing children, regardless of what the hearing mainstream believed "best" for them. They knew that the linguistic access of a visuo-gestural language was paramount, the most effective means for communication and sharing cultural history. Unlike many spoken languages, therefore, using ASL can be understood in a resistance context when used by Deaf people, an assertion of legitimacy in the face of ongoing oppression.

Before jumping into a discussion of d/Deaf oppression and interpreting in social justice organizing, the distinction between "deaf" and "Deaf" should be clarified. The use of the term "Deaf" describes a social, cultural, and political identity that is most often represented through the use of ASL. By contrast, "deaf" with a small d is the term used for those who do not hear. In other words, my 93-year-old grandmother who doesn't hear well any longer is "deaf." She knows no sign language, has no connection with the Deaf community, and still interacts with the world as a hearing person. My friend Erin, on the other hand, has about the same capacity to hear but is "Deaf" because of her use of ASL and her self-identification with the Deaf community.

ASL IS NOT ENGLISH

As important as clarifying the differences between "deaf" and "Deaf" is explaining to unfamiliar readers American Sign Language and how it differs from other spoken and signed languages. ASL, is commonly misunderstood by hearing people to be a modified version of English, or a kind of "English on the hands." American Sign Language is a natural language that evolved though its use by the Deaf community, just as spoken languages have evolved through use over time by hearing people. The signs used today are not always the same as those used a century ago, reflecting the ways languages develop over the generations. For example, the sign for "telephone" once looked like using the sort of old-fashioned phone with a separate ear and mouth piece. Today there are two ways to sign "telephone", one is to make the hand into the shape of a phone (a fist with the thumb and pinky out, much like how a hearing person would mime a phone) or to make the hand into the shape of holding a rectangular smart phone. Even more recently, signs for "Android" and "iPhone" have come into being, as the language grows alongside the culture.

The myth that ASL is a gestural version of English is bolstered by the presence and use of forms of signed English like Signed Exact English (SEE). These artificial sign languages were invented by hearing educators looking for a means of teaching spoken and written English to Deaf and hard of hearing students. These educators took signs from ASL and combined them with signs for verb endings, prepositions, and articles (which are unnecessary in ASL) to create a way to use signs to show English. It is often thought that while Deaf children benefit from visual language, using ASL in the classroom will prevent them from fully developing their English skills. This is presented as an alternative to teaching English as a second language after the students have fully developed their abilities in ASL. The result is a cumbersome and clunky means of communication that is often still challenging for students unfamiliar with English.

> **"A BROADER UNDERSTANDING OF OPPRESSION IS NECESSARY IF WE ARE INTERESTED IN CREATING A TRULY JUST AND EQUITABLE WORLD."**

Like other non-English speaking minorities, Deaf people in the United States face linguistic oppression on a number of levels. Many Deaf people use ASL as their native language, and may or may not be fluent in written English. As with all non-native English users, this can pose difficulties in reading and understanding things like medical forms, government documents, newspapers, and so forth, all presented in written English. As ASL has no written form, there is no simple option for providing a translated document. In some cases, an interpreter is brought in to render the form into ASL, but in most instances Deaf people are left without meaningful access to the information.

American Sign Language is thus both a means of communication and a form of political resistance. Hearing people in the US have long wielded language as a tool of oppression against Deaf people, demanding that they use spoken and written English and considering it superior to the natural language of Deaf people. As anarchists it is important for us to understand what ASL is, the role that ASL plays in Deaf organizing efforts, and its value to the Deaf populations of the US. Our analyses of oppressed groups should include not only an understanding of Deaf people as a minority, but also an understanding of the significance of linguistic access. It should further highlight for us the necessity for literary resources to be created in ASL through collaboration with Deaf organizers and Deaf translators. ASL is an integral part of Deaf social justice organizing and should be part of the overall efforts of anarchists to advance a more just and egalitarian society.

WHAT IS ASL INTERPRETING?

Put simply, ASL interpreting is the act of taking in a message in either ASL or English and then rendering it in the opposite language. ASL interpreters work in a wide array of environments, ranging from classrooms to doctors' offices, driving lessons to job trainings, and courtrooms to hospitals. Basically any place where a

Deaf and hearing person need to exchange information there may be an interpreter. Not all situations call for an ASL interpreter, and not all Deaf people always want an interpreter present. Some deaf people never learn ASL and therefore don't make use of interpreters. But when information needs to be conveyed between two people who don't share a language, an interpreter is often brought in to facilitate communication between them. This is as true for spoken language interpreting as it is for ASL interpreting.

The field of ASL interpreting dates back to the 1960's and the passage of legislation mandating the use of sign language interpreters in certain settings. Over the years, the profession has gone through four main "models" to describe and make sense of the work.[1] These began with the idea of interpreting as a charity done for helpless Deaf people, evolving to today's "bilingual-bicultural" model, which contends that hearing interpreters are members of both cultures and languages. Of interest to anarchists and other social justice activists is that none of the various interpretive models take into account the challenging dynamic of privilege and oppression at play in any interpreted interaction. Deaf people are an oppressed minority in the US (and elsewhere) whose right to use their native language and to access services and resources has often been limited at best. In any interaction between a Deaf and hearing person, there is imbalance of social privilege. The very presence of a hearing ASL interpreter simultaneously manifests the struggles Deaf activists have endured to achieve even a modicum of access and while reminding all participants of the imbalance of social power.

Interpreters make thousands of choices in every interpretation, all of which have an impact on the ways in which participants are able to advocate for themselves and their rights. For example, a hearing person may use the outdated and often offensive term "hearing impaired" and the interpreter may sign this as 'DEAF' (Becuase ASL has no written form, when an ASL sign is represented in written English it is typically capitalized. This is called a "gloss"). This prevents the Deaf participant from potentially correcting the hearing person directly because they may not be aware of the original word choice. The interpreter may not have thought at all about what to sign, or may have made a choice to use 'DEAF' rather than the sign for 'HEARING IMPAIRED.' Regardless, in so doing, they are disempowering the Deaf participant to a degree by altering the content of the original utterance. While small and seemingly insignificant, this example serves to illustrate the ways in which ASL interpreters are engaged in a dynamic of privilege and oppression that has yet to be fully acknowledged in the parlance of the field.

Some interpreters and authors, including myself, have brought forth a potential fifth model for interpreting, the "allyship" model. This model takes into account the social justice implications of ASL interpreting work and the functions of privilege and oppression at play in any interpreted interaction. While imperfect, it poses a new form of discourse for understanding the field and its relationship to the Deaf community. Deaf theorist and author MJ Bienvenue defines the concept as a process, rather than a destination, the acknowledging of privilege in how interpreters negotiate their boundaries and decisions in our work. It emphasizes partnership and collaboration with the Deaf community.[2] Of particular significance is the simple fact that all hearing ASL interpreters are, of necessity, hearing people and thus have hearing privilege. Like other forms of privilege, this means that we bring to the table our own assumptions, habits, and biases that may play out through our work. An "allyship" model attempts to account for such things in the field and make room for a more in depth discussion for the role of social justice thinking in ASL interpreting.

I have intentionally specified "hearing interpreters" in this text because, in addition to hearing people like myself who interpret between spoken English and ASL, there are Deaf interpreters who work alongside hearing interpreters to make interactions more equitable to a wider range of Deaf communicators. They often work with Deaf people who have limited language abilities perhaps due to an intellectual disability or because they come from another country that uses a different sign language. Deaf interpreters can have an important impact on the power imbalance of an interpreted situation. For example, imagine a Deaf patient meeting with a hearing therapist and a hearing interpreter. The Deaf patient is necessarily outnumbered. The fact that they are literally in the minority can leave them feeling less safe or open, potentially impacting the effectiveness of the therapy. When a Deaf interpreter is brought in, the ratio of Deaf to hearing people is balanced. One Deaf interpreter I work with said once that the Deaf interpreter is there for the Deaf person, while the hearing interpreter is there for the hearing person. The two interpreters are working together to make effective and equitable communication happen. Not only does the presence of a Deaf interpreter often improve the communication happening, it evens the scales and can create more comfort for the Deaf patient. I would argue that from a social justice vantage point Deaf interpreters are a critical aspect of re-centering Deaf people in the work and creating more equitable outcomes.

AUDISM & SOCIAL JUSTICE

The word that is used to describe the oppression faced by members of the Deaf and hard of hearing populations is "audism." This term is likely to be unfamiliar to hearing people. It was coined in 1975 by author and researcher Tom Humphries.[3] Audism is defined as a system of privilege and oppression based on the ability or inability to hear or act as one who hears. In short, audism is to Deaf people as racism is to people of color. This may seem like a forced analogy, given the history of colonialism and imperialism in the US and abroad. Some may contend that Deaf people, especially white Deaf people, have not been "colonized" in either a literal or figurative sense. But authors like Harlan Lane have made strong arguments describing the colonization of Deaf people. Deaf people and have long been subjugated to hearing norms and standards, forced into categories like "disabled" and deprived of their native language and culture. Even the language used to describe Deaf and hard of hearing people echoes the language used by colonists, being at best condescending and at worst outright derisive. Thus the analogy is more apt than it may seem, as will become clearer in the following paragraphs.

In "The Mask of Benevolence" author Harlan Lane draws a connection between European colonization of Africa with the relationship between hearing and Deaf people here in the United States. He notes that "Whenever a more powerful group undertakes to assist a less powerful one, whenever benefactors create institutions to aid beneficiaries, the relationship is fraught with peril."[4] Lane reviewed over three hundred books and articles on Deaf and hard of hearing people to gather a list of words used to describe the community by the professionals who serve them, including doctors, teachers, social workers, etc. His list found that the terms were almost entirely negative, making it clear that much of the literature is dealing more in stereotypes than actual realities, quite similarly to literature describing the colonized people of Africa. His list highlights the inherent paternalism of the hearing people who see themselves as "civilizing" Deaf people. Lane draws a connection with Foucault's notion of the "colonization of the body" by the state, an idea that should be of great interest to an-

> "DEAF PEOPLE AND HAVE LONG BEEN SUBJUGATED TO HEARING NORMS AND STANDARDS, FORCED INTO CATEGORIES LIKE "DISABLED" AND DEPRIVED OF THEIR NATIVE LANGUAGE AND CULTURE."

archists. Lane defines "audism" as "… the corporate institution for dealing with Deaf people […] the hearing way of dominating, restructuring, and exercising authority over the Deaf community."[5] He makes a clear connection between audism and the state: "The oppressive structural relations are the result of historical forces such as the appropriation of the body by the state […]; ethnocentrism and the formation of new states; the unequal distribution of wealth and power."[6]

Given that we live in a hearing world, it is easy to overlook the role of audism and audist thinking in our lives. Like racism, sexism, cissexism, and so on, audism manifests on a number of levels. It can be internalized, like when a Deaf person believes themselves to be innately less intelligent than a hearing person simply by virtue of being Deaf. Interpersonal audism occurs when a hearing person believes a Deaf person to be unintelligent because they don't use spoken English or don't write English well. It can be institutional, for example when a business refuses to interview a Deaf job candidate on the grounds that they don't want to pay for an interpreter. It can also be structural, for example when necessary information for advancement in one's job is accessed through hearing and therefore unavailable to a Deaf employee, like "water cooler" information gathered by chatting with fellow employees.

Audism is even further entrenched in philosophical notions of humanity, when the assumed definition of "human" includes the ability to use speech to communicate and the assumption that language must be spoken to be legitimate.[7] These ideas inform a host of services provided to Deaf and hard of hearing people, like when members of medical professions emphasize the use of hearing aids or cochlear implants for Deaf children or discourage hearing parents from using sign language at home.[8] Audism can even show up in how things are designed: in your home, your doorbell and smoke detector probably don't flash a light when they go off. Deaf people often pay to have such devices specially installed in their homes rather than the flashing light being the standard design of a doorbell or smoke detector. As another example, in my car, when I leave the headlights on a bell chimes to remind me to turn them off. This means that the designer did not have Deaf and hard of hearing people in mind when they designed their product. On more than one occasion a Deaf person with whom I was supposed to have a meeting had to reschedule because they mistakenly left their lights on overnight and had to wait for AAA.

While some of the examples above may seem minor, the prevalent audism in our society can—and often does—have life-or-death consequences for Deaf people. For example, Deaf people are routinely shot and killed for failing to respond to a verbal command by police. A recent—but certainly not unique—example is illustrative of this issue: In September 2017, a Deaf man in Oklahoma City was shot and killed by police officers who were looking for a vehicle involved in a hit-and-run. They approached him while he was on his porch holding a metal pipe and when he didn't comply with their request to drop it, which he couldn't hear, they shot him. Throughout the encounter his neighbors were repeatedly shouting "He can't hear! He can't hear!". He was known to carry the pipe around to deal with the feral dogs in the neighborhood. He had nothing to do with the hit-and-run. He was murdered by police because they failed to listen to his neighbors and jumped to the use of force rather than finding a means of communicating with him.[9]

Once arrested, Deaf people spend longer periods of time in detention prior to sentencing. For example, the organization Helping Educate to Advance the Rights of the Deaf, or HEARD, has found that Deaf people detained at Rikers Island in New York state are typically held longer than hearing peers with the same or similar charges.[10] Deaf suspects are routinely denied full communication access, including qualified ASL interpreters, leaving them unaware of the charges they face.[11] The Americans with Disabilities Act and section 504 of the Vocational Rehabilitation Act mandate the provision of ASL "interpreters" for Deaf people who are arrested, but, significantly, leave the definition of "qualified" to hearing law enforcement. "Interpreters" in these situations are not required to have any form of certification or education in interpreting.[12] This can lead to situations where a family member is asked to interpret for a Deaf suspect or witness, or worse, that a law enforcement professional who happens to know some ASL is called upon to interpret. Undoubtedly these are hardly unbiased people to interpret in these situations, even if they are fluent ASL users.

Once sentenced, Deaf people behind bars are routinely denied ASL interpreters for services including medical appointments and programs, despite these being violations of the Americans with Disabilities Act.[13] Furthermore, few prisons in the US provide videophones permitting Deaf sign language users to communicate with loved ones or attorneys, further isolating them and preventing them from accessing critical information about their case.[14] Worse still, Deaf incarcerated people may be punished for failing to respond to orders they didn't hear or not reporting to counts of which they were unaware.[15] Solitary confinement is often used instead of providing accommodations and protections, resulting in Deaf people spending long periods of time completely isolated, to devastating effects.[16] In general, the criminal justice system is rife with audism and audist practices. These situations can be life and death, leaving Deaf people unaware of the reasons for their arrest or their rights and, possibly, dead. Deaf activists and organizations have worked hard to improve their access to equitable justice but the gains are slow to come by. The hearing state is unwilling to adjust itself to be even minimally inclusive of Deaf and hard of hearing people.

DEAF ORGANIZING

In the early eighteenth century, schools for the Deaf that provided instruction in ASL began to emerge, providing Deaf people with far better access to education and in turn job opportunities.[17] Classrooms were often led by Deaf teachers, providing a significant source of employment for Deaf and hard of hearing people. But, in the later decades of the nineteenth century, hearing people decided that Deaf students should be instructed in spoken languages and that signing should be prohibited in schools. Schools for the Deaf had been an important site for the transmission of linguistic and cultural knowledge from Deaf adults to Deaf children. In response, Deaf people resisted, shifting the spaces in which signed languages were transmitted out of the public sphere and into the private sphere at Deaf gatherings and clubs.[18]

As a consequence of the hearing push to eliminate the use of ASL, over the course of the twentieth century schools for the Deaf began to decline. Deaf people had long been locked out of a number of fields and the loss of job opportunities provided through schools for the Deaf further diminished employment options for Deaf and hard of hearing people. Deaf activists didn't take this sitting down, however. They fought hard to gain access in the workplace and in larger society. During the 1960's and 1970's they worked with disability rights activists to improve accessibility in state-funded settings through the Vocational Rehabilitation Act of 1973.[19] The VR Act was the first to mandate that interpreters be provided in some situations where an organization received state money. As interpreters became increasingly available Deaf organizers pushed for their use in a wider variety of spaces, leading to the Americans with Disabilities Act, or ADA, which requires accessibility in all public accommodations, not just those receiving funds from the state.

With the advent of film in the early 20th century, Deaf people began to document their stories and language in order to preserve them in the face of a larger society that seemed set on eliminating them. George Veditz, a Deaf man, famously launched a project to gather up as much video as possible of sign language aiming to preserve it for posterity. Using the then-new technology of motion pictures, Veditz even suggested to Alexander Graham Bell, who was a staunch advocate for Deaf people learning to speak and becoming integrated into hearing society, that he create a device like the telephone using the new video technology. Nearly a century before the invention of the modern videophone, Veditz was pushing for its creation. Upon Veditz's efforts, the National Association of the Deaf raised money to create a number of films in the early twentieth century intended to preserve what Veditz saw as a deteriorating language. He described the hearing people trying to remove the use of signed language from the Deaf community as "Enemies of the sign language, they are enemies of the true welfare of the Deaf." He is well known for having signed in a recorded message in 1913: "We must use our films to pass on the beauty of the signs we have now. As long as we have Deaf people on earth, we will have signs. And as long as we have our films, we can preserve signs in their old purity. It is my hope that we will all love and guard our beautiful sign language as the noblest gift God has given to Deaf people."[20]

A survey of Deaf organizing must include the uprising that took place at Gallaudet University in the 1980s, commonly known as Deaf President Now. Gallaudet University is the world's only liberal arts university for the Deaf. It was founded in 1863 through a land grant and has grown ever since. Instruction is in ASL, and the university offers a wide array of programs for Deaf and hard of hearing students, ranging from associates to doctoral degrees. Despite having been in existence for over one hundred years at the time of Deaf President Now, the university had always been led by hearing people. In the 1980s, when it came time for the university to select a new president, another hearing person, a non-ASL user, was chosen by the board. The students and faculty rose up in resistance. They demanded that a Deaf person be named president and drew attention from around the world as they blockaded the campus until the board met their demands. They were successful, and a Deaf man was selected to lead the university. Two decades later a new uprising took place, this time pushing for a female Deaf president. Students, faculty, and staff demanded a Deaf person at the helm of this critical Deaf institution, and LGBTQ students and students of color rallied to make the university more inclusive of a wide array of Deaf identities.

> "THE HEARING STATE IS UNWILLING TO ADJUST ITSELF TO BE EVEN MINIMALLY INCLUSIVE OF DEAF AND HARD OF HEARING PEOPLE."

Deaf people have long had organizations focused on advocating for their civil and economic rights. The most prominent and longest standing is the National Association of the Deaf or NAD. Founded in the late nineteenth century, the NAD has played an important role in promoting the rights of Deaf and hard of hearing people. It has been involved in a number of campaigns for legislation and amendments to legislation to improve accessibility of resources and services to those who use ASL as their native language. In addition, the NAD was the first organization to provide certification for interpreters. This particular function was later merged with the Registry of Interpreters for the Deaf, the national professional organization for ASL interpreters like myself. Today, both bodies collaborate to provide certification exams and credentials for professional ASL interpreters.

A more recent Deaf advocacy organization is Deaf People United, fighting for social justice issues from a Deaf perspective. They often work with a new movement called We the Deaf People on lobbying for legislation and other actions to serve the needs of the Deaf and hard of hearing populations. HEARD, or Helping Advocate for the Rights of the Deaf, is a newer organization working with Deaf and hard of hearing people behind bars. HEARD is a volunteer organization whose accomplishments include successful advocacy for the installation of videophones in a number of state prisons. HEARD also tends to the more radical side, for example engaging in collaboration with abolitionist organizations like the Incarcerated Workers Organizing Committee in Rochester, New York, on a rally and noise demonstration in commemoration of the 45th anniversary of the Attica Uprising in September 2016.

In more recent years, Deaf and hard of hearing students on college campuses have been engaged in organizing work advocating for greater educational and language access in higher education. At the National Technical Institute for the Deaf (NTID), for example, students started a movement called Communication Access Now to improve their ability to fully engage with professors and staff. NTID is a college at the Rochester Institute of Technology, in western New York, and instruction is given in ASL. Many instructors, however, are not fluent signers. Deaf and hard of hearing students whose primary language is ASL have been frustrated by professors who are unable to lecture and interact in their native language. Although the university has a large Department of Access services providing interpreters for those students in non-NTID classes around the campus, they do not typically provide interpreters in NTID classes where instruction is ostensibly in ASL. On the other hand, Deaf and hard of hearing students who prefer spoken English have struggled to find interpreters to effectively work with them ensuring full access to their education. In 2016 these students rallied together to bring these issues to the attention of the administration of the college and make meaningful changes to how communication happens at NTID, successfully engaging with the president of the college and leading to a task force on the subject.

As Harlan Lane so clearly articulated, the state has played a central role in the perpetuation of audism in society, and its manifestations share common forms with other oppressions prevalent in US society. The hearing state has colonized Deaf people, or at least has continuously attempted to. Hearing anarchists would do well to develop our understanding of audism in our own lives and in our organizing, because it is yet another facet of how the state creates structures designed to maintain oppressive hierarchies upon its citizens.

DEAF ANARCHISTS?

What is missing from this survey of Deaf organizing is the lineage of Deaf anarchist efforts. This lack is likely not a reflection of a dearth of such work being done by Deaf people so much as a reflection of its lack of publicity and visibility. As a hearing anarchist interpreter I have yet to encounter Deaf anarchists. Some of the Deaf people with whom I work on social justice projects are certainly far-left in their politics and are receptive to anarchist thought, but none explicitly consider themselves anarchists. This is presumably a function of who I, the author, happen to know rather than a function of there being no Deaf anarchists. Searching the internet for "Deaf anarchist" has been fairly unfruitful. But it speaks to the need for hearing anarchists to open more lines of communication with Deaf organizers and revolutionaries and to cultivate real relationships with Deaf people who are engaged in movement work. It is clear from the survey above that there is a great deal of opportunity for hearing anarchists to connect with Deaf people and broaden the scope of our efforts. It is likely that there is a whole subset of the US Deaf population who is engaged in work that hearing anarchists would label "anarchist" but who don't call it such. By building ties with those doing the grassroots organizing we can expand our notion of social justice and connect with a whole new community and perspective.

INTERPRETING AND THE STATE

In the US, and elsewhere for that matter, accessibility has had to be won through hard fought legal battles by Deaf activists working with disability rights activists to persuade the state to mandate the accessibility of resources and employment. Prior to legislation like the VR Act and the ADA, there was no profession of interpreting as we know it today. Interpreting was a skill offered by hearing people who knew at least some sign, often a family member of a Deaf person, a teacher, or a priest/pastor.[21] These people were vetted by Deaf people, who shared information among themselves about who was a good choice to interpret. This centered Deaf people in the process of "training" and selecting interpreters, but there were few instances in which an interpreter was brought in. There was no funding or guarantee of services, meaning that interpreting happened far less often. With the heavy role the state has played in fostering even rudimentary accessibility, it is difficult to imagine accessible services in the modern context without state intervention.

The state's role in the provision of accessibility services poses a challenge to the notion of anarchist interpreting. It is arguable that without state intervention Deaf and hard of hearing people would have far less access to resources, jobs, education, and so forth. The fact that the state has, in this instance, been helpful does not mean it is the only way to ensure communication access. Nor does it mean it is the best way. To begin with, the state is run largely by hearing people. Few Deaf and hard of hearing people are involved in the state apparatus that provides for such services. Even if we consider the case of the nonprofits that work alongside the state, like the Registry of Interpreters for the Deaf or many interpreting agencies, we see a prevalence of hearing people in the position to make these important decisions.

Moreover, the shift away from the Deaf community having control over who is doing the work of interpreting, and towards hearing organizations and hearing people deprives Deaf people of a great deal of agency. It reinforces the Deaf-hearing oppression-privilege dynamic wherein Deaf people have limited control over the institutions within which they work and through which they receive services. When hearing people select other hearing people for interpreting work, they are less likely to have an intuitive sense of what is necessary contextually and linguistically. The hearing dominance of the field maintains a lesser status of Deaf people in the larger hearing world.

Additionally, the rights to accessible services have been won through legislation that considers Deaf people "disabled," despite the fact that many Deaf and hard of hearing people do not think of themselves as having a disability. The legislation that mandates the provision of ASL interpreters and other accessible communication lumps those rights in with the rights of people with disabilities to things like wheelchair ramps, wider doorways, etc. Furthermore, in order to receive any sort of state financial support, like Social Security, Deaf people must accept the label "disabled." The hearing state imposes onto them an identity in order to justify the most modest of benefits to compensate for the lack of income resulting from discrimination and limited opportunities. Deaf people have fought for and won the rights they have under the mantle of disability rights, whether or not they actually self-identify as people with disabilities. The state does not consider Deaf people members of a linguistic and cultural minority, rather, it classes them as people lacking in a normative bodily function, the ability to hear. This perspective shapes the way those rights are satisfied, and the legal arguments Deaf people can make when they contend they have been denied adequate accessibility.

> "DEAF PEOPLE HAVE FOUGHT FOR AND WON THE RIGHTS THEY HAVE UNDER THE MANTLE OF DISABILITY RIGHTS, WHETHER OR NOT THEY ACTUALLY SELF-IDENTIFY AS PEOPLE WITH DISABILITIES."

To illustrate the above: I often interpret in classrooms at a local community college. The Deaf students with whom I am working arrange for interpreting services and receive advisement through the office Services for Students with Disabilities. When they are looking for help with reading and writing in English—which is logical given that English isn't their native language—rather than being connected with ESOL (English Speakers of Other Languages) resources, they are placed in remedial reading and writing classes. They can't access the same kind of tutoring or other help available to their fellow non-native English users because all of the services for Deaf students come under the heading of "disability services" and are funded through different streams. Students with whom I have worked have expressed frustration at the inability to get the help they need. The assumption is that, because they're from the US, they are fluent users of English. The infrastructure and funding available to the college to cover the cost of interpreters and so forth is all channeled through disability services; were these students to be logically labeled as "ESOL" they wouldn't be able to get the other resources they might need or want to succeed in a hearing college environment like notetakers or captionists.

ALTERNATIVE APPROACHES

Being opposed to any sort of state apparatus, anarchists should be interested in new models for ensuring accessibility. In terms of the provision of services, we see simple examples of "anarchist interpreting" when interpreters either volunteer (work "pro bono", in the parlance of the field) or work in exchange for things other than money. For example, an interpreter may exchange interpreting services for other goods or resources, like help preparing taxes. Alternatively, they may offer it as a community contribution. For example, in Rochester, home to the largest per capita Deaf population in the country, all of the Pride Week events are interpreted by a team of volunteer professionals who are either LGBTQ or allies. In such cases, interpreters are willing to donate their time in the interest of making an event accessible to Deaf and hard of hearing community members. The fact is that for many organizations the cost of providing interpreting, particularly through an agency, is prohibitive, so the options are either volunteers or none.

But a trade or volunteer services aren't always feasible, and can't cover the wide array of situations in which an interpreter may be necessary. Some interpreters today work in informal collectives, groups of interpreters who network with each other and share jobs with one another. This brings us to an idea that is slowly coming into being: the interpreting cooperative. According to the International Cooperative Alliance, "Co-operatives are businesses owned and run by and for their members. Whether the members are the customers, employees or residents they have an equal say in what the business does and a share in the profits."[22] There are already a handful of ASL and spoken language interpreter cooperatives in existence with a variety of structures. These challenge the typical business approach used by interpreting agencies by utilizing a democratic decision making structure and shared governance model.

The sort of cooperative I might envision is akin to a grocery cooperative. Interpreters and the organizations using services would be members. Member organizations would pay monthly dues in exchange for a fixed number of hours of services. Dues would be sliding scale, allowing organizations with limited funds to still make use of services. This would make it possible for groups that otherwise aren't able to afford interpreters to better serve and connect with Deaf community members. Member interpreters would contribute a fixed number of hours to the co-op and the revenue from dues would be paid out equally. Deaf users of services would participate in the process of securing interpreters and be integral in the assessment of interpreter members. Any leftover dues funds not allocated to the interpreters or operating expenses would be shared with Deaf community organizations.

However, the co-op model only resolves some of the most obvious problems with the for-profit interpreting industry, and would itself be a non-profit, thus facing the same critiques of other non-profit entities. It also works within a capitalist system, operating as a business dealing in revenue, paying taxes, and so forth. Interpreter-members would expect a pay rate that is commensurate with their training, qualifications, and competitive with other payment options. Why would a highly experienced and certified interpreter take a potentially large pay cut with only the moral benefit to compensate for it? While many might agree that the model is ethically better, it doesn't make sense to expect interpreters to collectively decide that a potential decrease in pay is acceptable because it seems ethically better. This is especially true given that the RID Code of Professional Conduct, the document describing ethical behavior for its members, frames ethics as largely an issue of individual interpreters, rather than with regards to the field at large. In my experience, much of today's interpreter culture is intensely individualist and capitalist. The interpreting cooperative would thus need to fit itself into the capitalist expectations of current working interpreters and into the broader financial system, making it only a step in the direction of interpreting services returning to their more collectivist Deaf community roots.

Furthermore, the co-op model doesn't address the larger question of the state's involvement in services. After all, the reason the member organizations bring in interpreters would still often be because they are required to do so by law. It would be unreasonable to expect organizations and institutions to suddenly begin caring about Deaf accessibility simply because equitable access to resources is a good thing to do. Even if they do see the ethical and even anti-oppression value in accessible services, they may not be able to afford quality interpreters without financial support from the state to cover the cost of those services. Looking beyond the state requires us to employ our anarchist imaginations and envision a totally different society, one in which accessibility is understood to be an important part of how we organize our lives together.

ACCESSIBILITY IN ANARCHIST SOCIETY

In a non-hierarchical society committed to egalitarianism, we know that all voices would be important to the functioning of communities. There would still be a need for people to do the work of interpreting when Deaf and hard of hearing ASL users come together with hearing people who don't know ASL. In such a society, interpreting work would be one of the many contributions made by community members. Individuals fluent in ASL would share their skills as part of the functions necessary for community life.

Interpreting would not be the only way in which such a society would ensure full community engagement. For example, "writing" no longer needs to be in print. In our 21st century world it is increasingly possible to create documents in video formats, permitting Deaf people to compose and share texts in their native language. Among Deaf people the app Glide, for example, has become incredibly popular because it allows individuals to send video "text" messages easily and without storing large numbers of videos to their smartphones and eating up memory. Websites like YouTube and Vimeo have made it much easier for groups and individuals to post documents in video formats, and several Deaf news organizations have sprung up in recent years providing information and commentary in ASL and distributed via these sites and other social media platforms.

Work environments could be designed to best suit hearing and Deaf workers alike, something increasingly possible with technologies like videophones. Simple adjustments can be made to work environments like the elimination of cubicles and placing workspaces in a visually accessible set-up to improve Deaf and hard of hearing people's capacity to participate in group conversation and discourse. As a simple example, ASL-using classrooms are typically arranged in a circle so students can see each other. A similar approach can be applied to various work spaces. Services and resources would intentionally include the needs of Deaf and hard of hearing people, like ensuring that all smoke detectors and doorbells—not just the ones in places covered by the ADA—had flashing lights in addition to sounds. Broadly speaking, Deaf and hard of hearing ASL users would be seen as linguistic and cultural minorities who are part of the larger diversity of the community.

Education could be multilingual, with classrooms where instruction is provided in ASL for Deaf and hard of hearing signing students, rather than forcing them into mainstreamed classrooms where they access the information only through an interpreter. These classrooms would include hearing students who also use ASL, creating communities where more people can communicate in multiple modalities. As a result, in many situations where contemporary western society brings in an interpreter, there would be no need because more non-Deaf people would be able to use ASL. With more people knowing how to sign at least reasonably well, more of the interactions that today require an interpreter to be accessible would no longer need one. This would provide more opportunities for Deaf people, both in terms of spreading ASL throughout the community as well as making more room for them to be involved in a wide array of community activities as regular participants. Imagine a workplace where all workers know ASL, whether they're Deaf or hearing. The Deaf worker would be able to go to any meeting, participate in any chit chat, get any training, all without special arrangements or state oversight.

> "POST-REVOLUTIONARY SOCIETY DOESN'T NEED TO REINVENT THE WHEEL, WE SIMPLY NEED TO KNOW OUR HISTORY AND SHARE OUR KNOWLEDGE TO CREATE THE ACCESSIBLE WORLD THAT WE ENVISION FOR OURSELVES."

There is precedence for this: from the mid-1600s into the 1900s, Martha's Vineyard was home to an extensive Deaf population and its own flourishing sign language that pre-dated ASL. Nearly all the people who lived on the island, Deaf or otherwise, were able to use the native sign language. Deaf islanders were independent and full citizens of the island.[23] This is significant, because it demonstrates that a more accessible community, one wherein accessibility is part and parcel of how life is organized, is not only possible but has already been done.

Post-revolutionary society doesn't need to reinvent the wheel, we simply need to know our history and share our knowledge to create the accessible world that we envision for ourselves. Culturally and linguistically diverse communities can exist, indeed they already have. More people knowing basic ASL in communities with Deaf populations is as useful as more people being able to speak everyday Spanish. An anarchist society would still have interpreters who offer their skills to the community, but wouldn't need them in the simpler situations because visual language and communication strategies would be normalized. A radical commitment to accessibility means reconsidering our whole understanding of what it is to be "human" and adjusting our interactions accordingly. Crafting the society we envision just means thinking more broadly about how we connect with each other and challenging ourselves to get more creative.

CONCLUSION

On a very basic level, the takeaway here is that when anarchists organize events, rallies, and so forth, there should be interpreters. But it is about far more than that: Deaf people have been organizing for centuries, often using their native languages to subvert the narrative of "defective" or "impaired" imposed on them by the larger hearing world. From an anarchist vantage point, it is necessary to reframe our understandings of Deaf people and ASL such that they are in line with the language used by Deaf people themselves to describe who they are and their own efforts towards liberation. This is not about hearing people taking on the work of liberating Deaf people. Like white people involved in social justice efforts of people of color, or men involved in combating patriarchy, this is about hearing people recognizing our privilege, recognizing how the world in which we live and organize has been designed both intentionally and unintentionally assuming a hearing norm, and actively making changes. Working with Deaf people always involves hearing people checking in on our assumptions and pushing ourselves to learn more, to step back, and to expand our frame of reference for what "accessible" means. Working with Deaf people often—but not always—involves interpreters. For hearing anarchists new to what is often called the Deaf World interpreters are a necessary component of developing relationships with Deaf people. But they are only a part of the equation.

At its core, this essay isn't simply about how to get an interpreter for your next info session. It's about how to rethink accessibility such that it is woven into every event, every meeting, every interaction. It is about developing an anarchist praxis that understands radical accessibility as a necessary component of the larger revolutionary project. A revolution that leaves anyone behind is no revolution at all, and to leave out the decades of efforts made by Deaf people themselves towards their own liberation is not only ignorant, it would be cheating ourselves of new dimensions of what revolution could look like. This essay is only a beginning, intended to introduce a series of ideas and to foster thought. Real revolutionary activity will happen when we, anarchists, are able to effectively engage with and support the liberation of Deaf and hearing people alike to create the truly egalitarian society we seek.

This article was made possible by a generous grant from the Institute for Anarchist Studies and the wonderful Deaf community members who have guided me in my development as an interpreter and as an organizer.

ABOUT THE AUTHOR

Tristan Wright is a nationally certified professional ASL interpreter in Rochester, New York. He holds a bachelor's degree in ASL-English Interpretation from the National Technical Institute for the Deaf where he was awarded Outstanding Graduate for the class of 2014. He is also a member of the Black Rose Anarchist Federation and a prison organizer. His writing has been published in the *Empty Closet Newspaper* and the *Genesee River Rebellion*.

ENDNOTES

1. Janice H. Humphrey and Bob J Alcorn, *So You Want to Be an Interpreter: An Introduction to Sign Language Interpreting* (Seattle, WA: H&H Publishing Company, 2007), 171-185.
2. MJ Bienvenue, "Bridge to Allyship: Understanding Accountability as Sign Language Interpreters," *Street Leverage*, May 2017, available at https://streetleverage.com/live_presentations/bridge-to-allyship-understanding-accountability-as-sign-language-interpreters/ (accessed April 2017).
3. H-Dirksen L. Bauman, "Audism: Exploring the Metaphysics of Oppression," *Journal of Deaf Studies and Deaf Education* 9, no. 2 (2004): 239-46.
4. Harlan L Lane, *The Mask of Benevolence: Disabling the Deaf Community*, (San Diego, CA: Dawn Sign Press, 1999), 33.
5. Lane, 43.
6. Lane, 87.
7. Bauman, 241.
8. Bauman, 244.
9. James Doubek, "Oklahoma City Police Fatally Shoot Deaf Man Despite Yells of 'He Can't Hear,'" NPR The Two Way 9/21/17 available at https://www.npr.org/sections/thetwo-way/2017/09/21/552527929/oklahoma-city-police-fatally-shoot-deaf-man-despite-yells-of-he-cant-hear-you (accessed October 2017).
10. T.L. Lewis, "In the Fight to Close Rikers, Don't Forget Deaf and Disabled People," *Truthout*, April 6, 2017, available at http://www.truth-out.org/opinion/item/40136-in-the-fight-to-close-rikers-don-t-forget-deaf-and-disabled-people (accessed April 2017).
11. Lewis.
12. Sy Dubow, *Legal Rights: The Guide for Deaf and Hard of Hearing People*, (Washington, DC: Gallaudet University Press, 2000), 171-172.
13. Heyer V, US Bureau of Prisons Fourth Circuit, March 24th 2017; James C McKinley, "Judge Orders state to Provide Special Help to Deaf Prisoners," The New York Times (New York, NY) June 19, 1995.
14. McKinley, "Judge Orders state to Provide Special Help to Deaf Prisoners."
15. Lewis.
16. Lewis.
17. Carol Padden and Tom Humphries, *Deaf in America: Voices from a Culture* (Boston, MA: Harvard University Press, 2003), 7.

18. Padden and Humphries, *Deaf in America*, 31.

19. Dubow, 37.

20. George W. Veditz, "The Preservation of the Sign Language," *Deaf World: A Historical Reader and Primary Sourcebook*, ed. Lois Bragg, (New York: New York University Press,1913), 83-85.

21. Humphrey and Alcorn, 262.

22. "What Is a Cooperative?" International Cooperative Alliance, available at https://ica.coop/what-co-operative-0 (accessed October 2017).

23. Oliver W Sacks, *Seeing Voices: A Journey into the World of the Deaf*, (New York: Vintage Books, 1989), 28-29.

Art by Kevin Caplicki | Justseeds.org

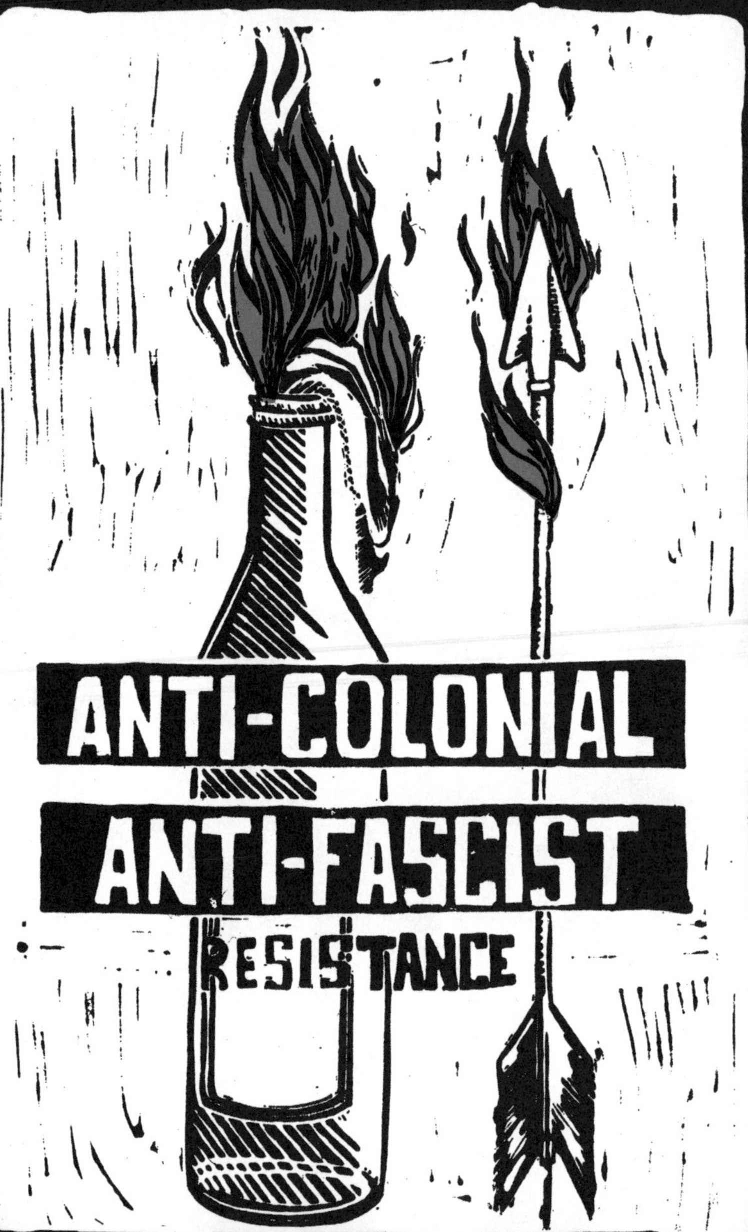
ANTI-COLONIAL
ANTI-FASCIST
RESISTANCE

BEYOND ANTIFASCISM, BUT NOT WITHOUT IT: A CALL FOR ONLINE CONTRIBUTIONS

THE *PERSPECTIVES ON ANARCHIST THEORY* COLLECTIVE

SINCE TRUMP'S ELECTION, FAScism has barged on to center stage, moving more brazenly into public space, mainstream media and public discourse than it has in decades. This renewed and emboldened presence of overt fascism has been met by an explosion of analysis and discussion about its history and politics, as well as the conditions necessary for its emergence. In equal proportion, growing attention is also being paid to the history and politics of anti-fascism. This anti-fascist response is welcome, and it is crucially needed.

Meanwhile, women, queer and trans people, and communities of color (particularly Black and Indigenous communities) who have been experiencing related forms of violence and raw hate for years have had full cognizance of the implications. Yet their analysis and resistance has not been accorded the same urgency and attention—even keeping in mind the major tectonic shifts initiated by Black Lives Matter and the Indigenous blockade movement against fossil fuel pipelines, as exemplified by Standing Rock.

When the first great global anti-fascist Popular Front emerged in the 1930s, Pan-Africanists and Asian anti-colonialists pointed out to their white leftist comrades and allies that what appeared unprecedented and alarming to them when it reared its head in Europe had long been familiar to those on the wrong side of the color line. The logics of white supremacy, and its institutions and systematized practices—including the brutal dehumanization (racialization, criminalization) of the "Other" and violent misogyny—had all been routine components of the apparatus of colonization, conquest, and dispossession. Thus, those logics, rhetorics, and practices had merely continued along their obvious trajectories by blossoming into fascism at home, where the shock was that they appeared close by and that they were visited upon "us," rather than acting far away, upon "them."

Black and brown revolutionaries declared (and proved) themselves ready and eager to step up and join the fight against fascism, while also insisting that these connections not be overlooked: that if Hitler, Mussolini, and Franco were confronted without simultaneously dismantling the British and French empires and the US racial regime, then the whole enterprise would be fatally flawed. Perhaps the present resurgence shows that they were right.

So what about now? What comparable connections need to be stated and foregrounded?

We need analysis and historical contextualization of fascism and anti-fascism, but we also need analysis and historical contextualization of their relationship to longstanding anti-racist resistance and decolonization efforts. Some of this has been done, but we need to pay more attention to this and further develop it. We need to talk about how institutionalized forms of white supremacy connect to the racism and imperialism of US world interventions, which in turn connect to systematic police murders and the mass incarceration of poor people and people of color. In order to provide a fuller perspective, and therefore a more effective ability to fight back, we need to understand what's different and distinct about the present moment, while also understanding its intersections and continuities. We need to hear more from those who have never stopped experiencing, recognizing, calling out, and fighting back against the not-so-dormant forces that have produced this latest crop of malevolent fascist blossoms.

We should appreciate those who have already laid out their analyses; they are essential to our struggle. Nevertheless, we also need to hear from the rest of the comrades, organizers, writers, and everyday folks. This is happening, and we want to amplify it. (For example, check out the work of Alexis Pauline Gumbs, Dilar Dirik, William C. Anderson and Zoé Samudzi, Robyn Spencer, the *Upping the Anti* collective, among others. We also refer readers to the work of Black anarchists such as Ashanti Alston, Lorenzo Kom'boa Ervin, Walidah Imarisha, and Kuwasi Balagoon.)

If you are writing, talking, and speaking out publicly and you want another forum for what you have to say, write us at PerspectivesonAnarchistTheory@gmail.com. Whether you have only an idea, a rough draft that needs work, or a fully formed and polished piece, we'd like to see what you're thinking and consider it for publication. Send it to us!

—*Perspectives on Anarchist Theory* collective, Institute for Anarchist Studies

THE ALT-CREEPS:
A REVIEW OF *AGAINST THE FASCIST CREEP* BY ALEXANDER REID ROSS (AK PRESS) AND *CTRL-ALT-DELETE* BY MATTHEW LYONS, ET AL (KERSPLEBEDEB)

GEOFF ROWAN

A FEW YEARS AGO A DEAR friend expressed his concern about what he perceived as a dangerous political and cultural turn to the right. "The Alternative Right, the men's rights activists, the Dark Enlightenment. All of these fascists are organizing and trying to build power. It scares me." In some arrogant attempt to posture as *very serious*, I scoffed at these reactionaries as "wingnuts confined to the internet," with no significance in "the real world." I was wrong.

We are experiencing a frightening and drastic rightward shift in the overall political climate, not only in the United States, but also throughout Europe and Asia as well. The 2016 presidential election and the events surrounding it have empowered and emboldened all of these tendencies and more. Formerly marginal sectors of the Far Right have stepped into the light of mainstream US politics. They have helped to build neo-fascist movements and elect a bullying right-wing populist to one of the most powerful positions in the world. From Trump, to Brexit, to LePen, to the Islamic state, to the Bharatiya Janata Party, the Far Right is on the move. They are attempting to organize for and to brutally impose their hierarchical and inegalitarian visions on society. I have since apologized to my friend.

I don't, however, think that my opinion was especially unique. Rather, I expressed a common view among folks on the radical Left. I argued for years that while fascists and the Far Right should certainly be opposed, they represented a far smaller threat to the lives and well-being of people of color than did the police, the prison system, and other institutions of official society. I am by no means the only one who held this position. Nor was I completely wrong. However, my complacency was sorely misplaced. It was, consciously or not, rooted in a view that saw social relations as stable and which failed to comprehend the total social, political, economic, and ecological crisis that we inhabit.

In this moment, those of us who seek to build a free and just world would do well to study our enemies and understand their politics, strategies, and history. Two recent books attempt to examine the history and politics of the insurgent Far Right: Alexander Reid Ross's *Against the Fascist Creep* and the anthology *Ctrl-Alt-Delete* published by Kersplebedeb.

Clocking in at almost 400 pages Reid Ross's tome is by far the more ambitious project. *Against the Fascist Creep* is an attempt to tell the history of insurgent fascist politics and their complicated relationship with the Far Left.

Throughout his book Reid Ross focuses more on the ideology of fascism as a revolutionary movement than on the operations and policies of fascism in power. Reid Ross starts by looking at populist tendencies of North American "Manifest Destiny" and the emergence of anti-elitist ideologies that remain deeply racist and authoritarian. From these roots, he looks at the explosion of radical and militant right-wing politics following the First World War. In the wake of that catastrophe, Europeans developed ideologies and built movements to make sense of a chaotic and unjust world and to change it. Anarchists and Marxists led revolutions and rebellions across the continent. In opposition to, but also sometimes influenced and inspired by these left-wing ideologies, more authoritarian and nationalist politics emerged; from "national syndicalism" to Italian Fascism, to German National Socialism. Amidst the chaos of power structures crumbling, radical movements splitting, and struggles over power and principles, fascism emerged in opposition to both the exploitation of capitalist modernity and the universalism of Marxist communism.

Following a lengthy engagement with the life and thought of fascist occultist Julius Evola, Reid Ross discusses the emergence of the European New Right (ENR) in the 1960s. Fueled by resentment in the face of decolonization, the ENR attempted to rebuild insurgent right-wing politics to fit the postwar reality. Drawing on the work of Italian Communist (and anti-fascist) Antonio Gramsci, these activists and intellectuals prioritized cultural transformation in the place of an immediate struggle for political power. They also tended to minimize explicit biological racism, in favor of a less alienating stress on cultural integrity and self-determination. Finally, while initially reacting against decolonization, they appropriated the revolutionary politics of their time, positioning themselves as radicals fighting for the liberation and self-determination of European people against the imperialism of US capitalism and Soviet state socialism. Reid Ross goes on to discuss various other Far-Right and fascist movements: Nazi skinheads from London, England to Portland, Oregon; National Bolshevism and radical nationalisms in Russia and the Ukraine; and now, the Alt-Right which helped sweep Donald Trump into power.

Reid Ross's book is important in that it touches on some significant yet often under-examined aspects of fascism. Instead of seeing Right and Left as simplistic opposites, he is willing to think about them inhabiting a more complex relationship. While Marxist and anarchist leftists have generally understood fascism to be the most authoritarian and violent form of capitalist rule, Reid Ross takes seriously fascism's radical, even revolutionary, opposition to capitalist modernity. From "national syndicalists" active following the First World War to "Nazi Maoists" in the 1960s, the author conveys how complicated and confusing this political terrain is.

The line between Left and Right, between communist and fascist, is often far from clear, leaving us with the difficult work of clarifying our own values and politics. The distinction between Right and Left is not always obvious. Throughout history the record has been complicated. From Bakunin to Mussolini and from Stalin to Metzger, insurgent anti-imperialism has intermingled with vitriolic anti-Semitism and racism on both the "Right" and "Left." The Far Right is both our competitor in this period of social crisis and a danger that can destroy the liberatory potential of our own movements from within if we fail to clearly draw political lines that distinguish our radicalism from theirs.

Unfortunately, *Against the Fascist Creep*, while hinting at important insights and essential questions, often fails to live up to its promise.

Reid Ross's attempt to understand fascism as a process is useful in helping us avoid dogmatic attachment to fixed definitions. However, he does tend to define every social, political, cultural, or spiritual trend he doesn't like as being fascist, or at least tainted by it. In a denunciatory tour of the impurities of the political spectrum, Reid Ross attacks everyone from Deep Ecologists to class struggle anarchists, accusing them of enabling the right, sometimes citing evidence and sometimes not. In identifying a "fascist creep," he is too quick to resort to a casual guilt-by-association in a constant search for enemies, mistaking a moralist purity for the kind of political clarity we need to fight and win.

The danger of a "fascist creep" influencing and poisoning both society as a whole and our left-wing movements is very real. From casual anti-Semitism to macho fetishization of violence, the Left too often shares values and politics with the radical Right. This must be resisted and opposed, but doing so requires real humility, self-criticism, and a commitment to political clarity that cheap self-righteousness cannot provide. A real examination of the "fascist creep" would involve something more than a hunt for enemy infiltrators in our otherwise good movements; it would require confrontation and struggle with our own limitations and weaknesses.

Too often throughout the text, Reid Ross fails to engage fascist politics as deeply as he could, opting rather to denounce and ridicule them. If we could defeat fascism by proclaiming our own superiority, this practice would serve us well. But real politics is not just about being right; it's about winning. We need to develop the resources and forces to defeat fascists in the streets. Books should help us understand our enemies, what they think, and how, and why. Moralistic posturing, while it may feel good for both author and reader, doesn't really help. The purpose of political analysis is not to distinguish between "good guys" and "bad guys" like a ten-year-old watching *STAR WARS*. Instead, we need the nuance and sophistication to actually understand the complexities of our world, our movements and our enemies in order to be able to successfully fight and win.

Finally, the writing itself is poor and confusing. Sometimes this is a result of needlessly academic big words. At other points it's just sloppily crafted paragraphs, which change the subject without transitions. At its worst *Against the Fascist Creep* feels like 400 pages of name-dropping, the author simply referencing all of the obscure thinkers and projects he knows of, strung together with convoluted prose.

In contrast to Reid Ross's meandering volume, the collection *Ctrl-Alt-Delete*, published by Kersplebedeb, is quick, clear, and to the point. At fewer than 125 pages, this book pulls together some useful and timely documents, which reflect on the political moment of Trumpism and the insurgent movements he rode to power.

The collection begins with the title essay by longtime anti-fascist researcher and writer Matthew Lyons. "Ctrl-Alt-Delete" is a fifty-page report in which he seeks to familiarize the reader with the history and ideology of the "Alt-Right." Beginning with its roots in both old school "paleoconservatism" and the European New Right, Lyons explains how intellectuals like Richard Spencer built a political milieu by synthesizing different strains of right-wing nationalism and internet culture. He then goes on to examine some of the different tendencies within the Alt-Right.

White nationalism and racism have been core to this political project with its hip rebranding of neo-Nazism, white supremacy, and anti-Semitism. Lyons, however, also discusses the gender politics of the Alt-Right, pointing to its roots in and connections with the online culture of anti-feminist backlash, from "Gamergate" to "pick-up artists." Also significant in this regard is the "male tribalism" of Jack Donovan and the Wolves of Vinland, who seek to establish male supremacist resilient communities autonomous from multicultural capitalist modernity. Other forces include right-wing anarchists who seek to resist state authority in favor of decentralized "tribalism," and "neoreaction," an ideology spawned from tech CEOs seeking philosophical justifications for their fantasies of corporate feudalism.

Finally, Lyons examines the relationship between the Alt-Right and Donald Trump. Many sought to use the Trump campaign as an opportunity to push their politics within a broader arena, and their interventions injected new levels of violence and cruelty into American electoral politics. Lyons' report is concise, clear, and extremely useful in giving a rundown of who the Alt-Right are, where they come from, what they believe, and what their role is in this historical moment. I suspect that this report will stand as the go-to on the subject for some time, and Lyons' recent book *Insurgent Supremacists* will likewise be necessary reading.

"The Rich Kids of Fascism" by It's Going Down is another attempt to analyze the Alt-Right. The focus here is on the class character of the movement. They argue that unlike other forms of fascist and right-wing politics, the Alt-Right is a class-elitist movement. They also point to the weaknesses of the Alt-Right as being an internet phenomenon without any demonstrated ability to fight for its politics in the streets. While this may well have been true at the time the piece was written, that certainly seems to be changing, and the fact that anti-fascist forces have been losing street fights over the last couple years should humble us. Overall, while the piece has some useful and interesting points, there is a definite tendency toward triumphalism, and self-righteous posturing. The macho chest-thumping of "we ain't afraid of no memes" may feel good and may psych us up as we get ready to hit the streets, but it doesn't actually help us make sense of the world or the enemies by whom we have too often been defeated.

K. Kersplebedeb's "Black Genocide and the Alt-Right" looks at the racial politics of the Alt-Right and argues that, though it has been less addressed than its sexism or anti-Semitism, anti-Blackness is at the core of the movement's politics. That's a good point, but the article is too short. In a historical moment when we are witnessing the emergence both of militant fascist and Black Liberation movements, the relationship of these phenomena is of the utmost importance for radicals. Kersplebedeb is right to point out the antagonism, but unfortunately does little more.

Finally, Bromma's "Notes on Trump" is an attempt to understand the 2016 election in the broader historical context, viewing Trump's victory as a response to capitalist crisis and a rejection of neoliberal globalization and neocolonial multiculturalism in favor of right-wing nationalism. Following real victories by anti-racist and anti-colonial liberation moments, capitalism shifted and made space for figures and forces from the African National Congress in South Africa to Barack Obama in the United States to step forward and administer global exploitation. Bromma suggests that we are currently seeing the repudiation of such "progressive" rainbow imperialism. Instead we are now faced with more open white supremacy and a chaotic and violent world situation.

We are in a period of crisis and upsurge where political categories are being rapidly undone and remade. The labels and genealogies that folks claim may matter much less than the content of their politics and what their practice looks like. Distinctions between anarchism and Marxism may matter far less than one's concrete commitment to building antiauthoritarian political culture or rooting one's politics in working class life. At this juncture of fear, confusion, crisis, and opportunity, it is unclear where new political forces will emerge. But if the history Reid Ross presents teaches us anything, it is that we must be on our guard and take great care in seeking political clarity. In this chaotic "marketplace of ideas" (particularly in the internet age), where every tendency from Democratic Confederalism to Marxism-Leninism-Maoism to Pan-Secessionism to National Bolshevism is on offer, the next fascist threat, the next praxis of terror and extermination, can appear from anywhere, from our enemies' midst or from our own.

The Trump administration and the Alt-Right are shifting and shattering official politics with its lies of progress, multiculturalism, and civility. Stability and peace are not on the table, but transformation is certainly on the horizon. Both Reid Ross's and Lyons' interventions are important reminders that the Left are not the only ones who can benefit from instability, and that the transformations ahead are as likely to be full of horror as they are to lead us to freedom.

ABOUT THE AUTHOR

Geoff lives in Portland, Oregon, where he (occasionally) works on the journal *Red Skies at Night*. He is the parent of a three-year-old who thinks that "singing protests" are "a little bit fun" but "fire protests" are "too scary."

Above: Kevin Caplicki | Opposite: Nicolas Lampert | Justseeds.org

PROTEST

ORGANIZE

OCCUPY

RESIST

STRIKE

SHUT IT DOWN

TACTICS OF RESISTANCE AND STRATEGIES FOR ORGANIZING:

A REVIEW OF *GUERRILLAS OF DESIRE: NOTES ON EVERYDAY RESISTANCE AND ORGANIZING TO MAKE A REVOLUTION POSSIBLE* BY KEVIN VAN METER ((IAS/AK PRESS) AND *HEGEMONY HOW-TO: A ROAD MAP FOR RADICALS* BY JONATHAN MATTHEW SMUCKER (AK PRESS)

SHANE MCDONNELL

Throughout *Guerrillas of Desire*, Kevin Van Meter tells the reader that as "guerrillas" we need three things to build a counter-movement/society to the prevailing one: solidarity, communication, and mutual aid. Though on paper these three recommendations may appear obvious to well-read leftists, Van Meter, by using an array of historical examples, outlines the lived experiences of such guerrillas. In his book he looks at African slaves in the US, and European peasants and workers, both at the onset and in the infancy of capitalism. For instance, if African slaves in the US are planning to run away, adequate lines of communication are required between fellow slaves, leading up to and during the escape. This necessitates a strong sense of solidarity so no one snitches to the master and causes further suffering. Mutual aid is also necessary, whether it be physical, emotional or by omission, such as by being silent and not divulging the runaways' plans. On top of these three necessities, Van Meter gives a list of historical and potentially contemporary means of combating the prevailing system: theft, sabotage, go-slows, wildcat strikes, feigning illness, arson, suicide and assassination (these final three are very much associated historically with slavery, and in no way are promoted/encouraged). These methods are serious means of disrupting capitalism and the bosses' profits. They should not be taken on lightly.

Van Meter outlines how these tactics can be applied in different contexts, and how some are better than others, given the specific situation. Risking one's means of employment or the treatment of one's fellow workers by sabotaging work equipment owned by the boss, without having the appropriate lines of communication and strong solidarity, may not be the most strategic means of fighting the system, for example. It is in these specific lived experiences that the reader can see the blunders and successes of theories. In reality there are always consequences, and tactics need to be supported by communication, solidarity and mutual aid, as Van Meter continuously points out. There is a reason these tactics (and the necessity for these three things) recur throughout the text. Van Meter is showing their effectiveness, but also their gravity, and the requirement to use them within a specific context. Further, Van Meter demonstrates how tactics change over time, from slavery in the US to more contemporary contexts.

Guerrillas of Desire discusses the historical strategies of those who also lived in two other times and spaces beyond the experience of slavery, namely capitalism's infancy in Europe, and the late 20th century in Europe and the US. In these three historic periods, Van Meter shows how disrupting the capitalist system while maintaining solidarity, communication and mutual aid, forms and strengthens the working class (in which he includes slaves, homemakers and others, though acknowledging their clear differences). Van Meter informs us that African slaves in the US (re)constructed an ethical framework whereby stealing from their owners was acceptable but stealing from one another was not (79). An understanding of the above ethical framework remains necessary today and requires a similar inflexible solidarity between workers regarding snitching. This example gives us an ethical framework for living with one another under different forms of oppression. We are also told that as female slaves were usually allowed access to the master's kitchen, they were typically the ones responsible for poisoning their masters, the masters' families, or sometimes fellow slaves as a way to escape their servitude (79). Of course such murders ought to be viewed as examples of extreme desperation, implying the levels of cruelty such systems of oppression employ.

Turning to capitalism's infancy in Europe, Van Meter discusses peasants, enclosures of communal lands, and witch trials that removed women's traditional place in society and any authority they had. Interestingly, aspects of both land enclosures and the disempowerment of women overlap, and Van Meter illustrates this perfectly. As lands were being enclosed, forests began to be regulated. Taking wild foods and timber from the forest quickly became a crime punishable by "proto-police forces" (85). At the same time, the educated classes created schools in order for so-called 'proper' forestry and horticultural means and methods to be propagated, thus eradicating local and traditional knowledge and practices. Van Meter depicts what may have been a typical occurrence at the time of Europe's witch trials: bar women used to collect nettles as a bittering agent for beer, and also had the power to kick drunks out (thus controlling men's access to alcohol). However, as nettle picking was outlawed while the use of hops, which centered around men's work, was introduced, bar women lost their jobs (85). Thus Van Meter illustrates for the reader the overlapping aspects of oppression, i.e. racism, patriarchy, capitalism and varying state apparatuses. Further, he shows how such systems of oppression live with the oppressed throughout their day-to-day lives.

"The complexity of resistance calls attention to the importance of everyday life as a site of struggle but also the need for inquiry, intervention, and theorization" (129).

The final period of Van Meter's study covers the late 20th century. However, Van Meter begins the chapter by way of a very brief overview of social organizations in England in the centuries leading up to the 20th, e.g. the London Corresponding Society (1792-1799) which sought to make Parliament more responsive to working class needs. It is in the latter half of the 20th century that Van Meter outlines the activities of organizations and unions, of protests and groups making demands. In the 1960s and 1970s Van Meter points to slowdowns and strikes as a popular form of disruption and resistance. Sabotaging work equipment becomes a popular means of disrupting capitalism and the systems of oppression. Van Meter briefly mentions the evolution of workplace surveillance, from guards to CCTV cameras and body scanners, as theft becomes a successful means of resistance and disruption. Further, exodus as a means of disruption and combat becomes a tactic, i.e. workers leaving an area for better treatment, wages and other advantages elsewhere. An interesting tactic Van Meter discusses as being particularly successful is "counter-planning," whereby an alternative plan is implemented to accomplish tasks, take breaks and transfer power away from management. "Initial gripes [e.g. being made to work when it is too hot] amass into collective grievances, which in turn sparks further action" (123).

Van Meter ends his book by discussing organizing in the 21st century. He discusses the decline of unions under the rise of neoliberalism whereby non-profits replace former state functions and unions. Van Meter is concerned over this development as, he points out, "Non-profit social services are not as accountable to public pressure campaigns or demands of individual recipients as government-provided services are, and hence it is a conservative force" (141). On top of this, he examines the rise of affinity groups and collectives during the Cold War and in the contemporary 21st century. Van Meter points out that modern affinity groups differ greatly from affinity groups of the past, such as during the Spanish Revolution, as they possess limited contact with neighbors and other workers, which creates a sense of isolation and failure in an atmosphere that does not have ongoing public engagement and demonstrations. "Currently affinity groups and collectives, [...] community-based organizations, non-profits, and business unions, are ill equipped to orient themselves toward resistance taking place in everyday life" (151). Van Meter ends by discouraging the use of "false dichotomies," i.e. spontaneous vs. organized, underground vs. aboveground, conscious vs. unconscious, etc. According to Van Meter, contemporary organizing groups, from non-profits to unions, assume that the working class is not resisting and thus need to be encouraged to do so. Van Meter objects by way of the evidence gathered in his book and insists such leaders (of non-profits and unions) "inquire into, amplify, circulate, and propagate" the refusal to work and the resistances and struggles happening everyday by people in their lived experiences (151).

HEGEMONY HOW-TO

Complementing *Guerrillas of Desire*, Jonathan Matthew Smucker's *Hegemony How-To* discusses movements and criticizes terms such as *activism* and *activists* as meaningless titles that do not necessitate activity. He cites the mass increase in the use of such "content-less" terms despite a lack of visible and physical engagement and empowerment of communities (33-4). Smucker sees online petitions, which do not engage masses in ways that are as visible and disruptive as protesting, as the popular form of activism nowadays (33-8). There is a silent judgement over how effective such invisible and nondisruptive "activism" can truly be.

The Occupy Wall Street (OWS) movement is also critiqued and analyzed. Having been a member of OWS, his observations are particularly interesting and useful. Smucker makes it clear that OWS was an important movement that refocused the national narrative and gave the masses a new vocabulary to confront their oppression, e.g. "We are the 99 percent." A widespread and useful criticism of OWS is its lack of leaders, as well as what appears to be an impractical insistence on consensus decision-making. By not having or allowing leaders to exist, hidden unofficial leaders emerged. As Jo Freeman explains in her influential essay *The Tyranny of Structurelessness*, "As long as the structure of the group is informal, the rules of how decisions are made are known only to a few and awareness of power is limited to those who know the rules. Those who do not know the rules and are not chosen for initiation must remain in confusion, or suffer from paranoid delusions that something is happening of which they are not quite aware." On top of this, insisting on consensus decision-making, though not necessarily a bad method of making decisions if structured and facilitated well, led to impractical marathon meetings averaging six to eight hours long. (Smucker does not offer an in-depth analysis of the structure or facilitation of these meetings.)

Smucker, to his credit, encourages movements not to shy away from having leaders or possessing power, as he asserts that the Left in the US does. Though Smucker does not explore this, there is an obvious difference between having power in a protest, or civil rights or labor movement, than having power in an oppressive system. (Van Meter differentiates these two types of power well by calling the former *potentia* and the latter *potestas* (30)) Contrary to the leaderlessness of OWS, Smucker encourages groups to be "leaderful," whereby everyone has a role and is in a sense a leader of sorts. In contrast to the OWS movement, Smucker praises the "leaderful" organization of the Black Lives Matter movement as not being afraid of having leaders and cultivating leadership skills in the face of difficult challenges, while still decentralizing power and control (185n16). Though only a brief mention, Black Lives Matter's organizational approach and cultivation of leaders ought to be looked to more than the example set by OWS.

Smucker continually emphasizes having a strategy and a strategic plan over and/or alongside developing group identity. His discussion on prefigurative politics (chapter 4) outlines his fear that, though complementary to a strategic politics, prefigurative politics have replaced the idea of having a strategy (122). Smucker defines prefigurative politics as a politics that "seeks to demonstrate the better world it envisions for the future in the actions it takes today" (266). Having said that, Smucker's concept of prefigurative politics appears to reflect his experience in the OWS movement: he does not accept that prefigurative politics genuinely happened in the OWS movement, except as a performance (123). "I situate 'prefigurative politics' squarely within the *life of the group*, and I contrast it with the *strategic politics* that groups engage in to achieve ends beyond their own existence. I do not accept prefigurative politics' account of itself. In many instances, I do not even accept that it is politics at all" (123). Smucker criticises any political movement, in this case OWS, that is "only" made up of elements such as free libraries, people's kitchens, mic-checks and sparkle fingers, the final two being notable in the OWS movement (122).

Frustratingly, Smucker seeks and insists on strategies, yet, does not see the long term strategy inherent in such social organizing tools like free libraries and people's kitchens. Earlier in his book, Smucker acknowledges that OWS refocused the national narrative and gave the masses a new vocabulary to confront their oppression, e.g. "We are the 99 percent." Despite this, Smucker is later unable to see how other aspects of OWS can have a similarly wide impact and encourage people to set up alternative forms of distribution, e.g. the same free libraries and people's kitchens Smucker does not see as an effective political engagement. Smucker wants mass political engagement but appears to only want a certain type that is more legitimate and proper than others. "I am neither against manifesting our vision and values in our internal organizing processes, nor staging actions that put these visions and values on public display; my critique, rather, is of the notion that such practices can somehow substitute for strategic engagement at the level of political power" (122). These supposed strategic engagements that are being substituted are never noted or explored.

On the issue of strategy and tactics particularly, Van Meter's *Guerrillas of Desire* and Smucker's *Hegemony How-To* overlap and ought to be read together. Smucker also, aware of the unpopularity of his views regarding strategy and prefigurative politics, suggests smarter and better branding by way of attracting new members, organizing and pushing one's message (200-207). "The right seems to have learned more lessons of political strategy from the civil rights movement than the left has!" (36). Smucker's point regarding public relations is that if it successfully works for advertizing and capitalism, surely it can work for political movements. As he points out, corporations have invested large sums of money in psychological studies; analyzing this data might reveal something useful for our own campaigns, if even how to win over so-called middle ground undecideds. A cautionary note would suggest that it would be counterproductive if such pragmatism resulted in assimilation by the very system one seeks to disrupt and destroy. If a campaign or movement becomes purely about branding and less about effecting change, a failure of sorts has taken place. Having said that, Smucker notes this and cautions against relying heavily on such PR campaigns without face-to-face public encounters. "While we shouldn't simply mimic corporations' marketing techniques, we do have to navigate the same cognitive universe that they navigate, and it behooves us to study this terrain – we should never be too proud or too pure to learn things from our opponents" (207).

It is interesting to note that the book's publisher (AK Press) states that some of Smucker's politics include strategies they would not advocate. It struck me as worthy of mentioning here as *Guerrillas of Desire* is also an AK Press publication, co-published with the IAS, yet does not contain any similar warning. One can assume that AK Press's cautionary paragraph is an atypical disclaimer. Though Smucker describes himself, or at least his younger self, as an anarchist, he never references anarchists or anarchist theories or principles. Two thinkers who are continually referenced are Antonio Gramsci and Chantal Mouffe. While Mouffe and Gramsci have arguments, criticisms and ideas to offer, a tone is subtly set given the lack of anarchist writers cited. For example, throughout, Smucker discusses solidarity and reaching out to different communities, but says nothing about Kropotkin's idea of cooperation, despite Kropotkin's coming to similar conclusions which may have been useful here (chapter 8). Smucker disputes class-only analysis, implying the need for intersectionality. However, though mentioning intersectional categories (e.g. race, gender, sexual orientation, etc.), Smucker does not discuss or mention the term 'intersectionality' (241). Interestingly, Slavoj Žižek is referenced twice but theorists like Howard Zinn, Noam Chomsky and David Graeber are not. Further, Martin Luther King is cited often with an implicit idolization, yet other Left Black leaders and theorists, such as Malcolm X and Angela Davis, are noticeably absent.

Regarding reaching out to different communities, Smucker speaks very well on this: "A fledgling movement that attempts to attract only individuals [...] one at a time, will never grow fast enough to effect big systemic change" (35). He puts forth an array of helpful tactics from the obvious to the less obvious. Smucker warns of the in-crowd aesthetic that can accidentally form when the same people are always present at group meetings (194-200). Not only might this create an implicit hierarchy, it may also be off-putting to potential members with similar political leanings and concerns. Further, he cautions readers on several occasions not to alienate potential allies by cultivating too much of an in-group identity that fosters a sort of elitist image. We are warned that some of our quirky group dynamics, which can be good for creating better group cohesion and bonding, can seem incomprehensible and off-putting to those who may wish to join. While image is important, consistently having a certain image further alienates those who wish to join us but fall outside that supposed category, e.g. if group spokespeople and leaders consistently appear to be white, cisgender, and middle class. Others in more marginalized communities might feel unwelcome or noticeably and uncomfortably different. Alleviating this concern is important, especially when a certain cause unites us wherein skills and action, not image and identity, are what ought to matter.

On top of this, Smucker notes that compared to right-wing groups, leftist circles are complicated and nuanced. Unlike right-wing groups, we are not opposing a caricatured and simplified demonic version of one particular category of people. In left-wing groups there is a lot of discussion around structures, theories, thinkers, and nuanced points of view. Smucker warns that this expectation of knowledge for newcomers can seem daunting and further cement the perspective of in-crowd group dynamics (242). As well, the language used to explain this issues or the purpose of the group itself may be unhelpful if couched in academic and/or typically left-wing vocabulary. As an obvious but often forgotten remedy, Smucker recommends that we approach others in terms of their world where they are, with images and a vocabulary they can understand. This necessitates having good facilitators at meetings, though Smucker uses the term "leader": "Without strong internal bonding, group members will lack the level of commitment required for serious struggle. But without strong external bridging, the group will become too insular...to forge the kind of alliances that are essential to winning meaningful changes in society. Good leaders must learn to perform this extraordinary balancing act." (98)

CONCLUSION

While I recommend both books, as both are very informative, *Guerrillas of Desire* is more enjoyable due to its content. It is shorter and reads very much like a history book. Van Meter discusses each time period without being too long or too dry. *Hegemony How-To* is longer, though not excessively so, and is very much focused on tactics and strategy which, though important, can sometimes read as boring and make it appear lengthier than it is. Due to its content, it is much easier to disagree with Smucker's *Hegemony How-To* than with the more historical discussion in *Guerrillas of Desire*. Having said that, *Hegemony How-To* is important to read, as it refocuses the reader on the necessity of having a strategy and forming tactics to accompany one's goals. Smucker portrays the Left in the US as naive, shy, and weakened. Coupled with Smucker's seeming lack of knowledge about anarchism, and certainly his lack of discussion of intersectionality, one wonders about Smucker's intended audience. As a side note, Smucker does not explicitly criticize the state, whereas Van Meter continually critiques the state and its involvement in oppression and capitalism. Nevertheless, Smucker succeeds in reminding the reader about appropriate ways of reaching out to other communities, and the failing tactics of the Left in the past. Both *Hegemony How-To* and *Guerrillas of Desire* are especially important for anyone involved in groups and/or campaigns. Read both but understand the differences between the radical and reformist approaches taken by each author.

ABOUT THE AUTHOR

Shane McDonnell is a political activist in the Republic of Ireland. He received a master's degree in Philosophy and Public Affairs in University College Dublin (UCD). Currently he is a member of the Abortion Rights Campaign (ARC), campaigning to grant free, safe, and legal access to abortion services for pregnant people. Shane's main philosophical interest is Nietzsche. However, since adopting a libertarian-socialist political philosophy and vegan lifestyle, his interests have grown to include the prison-industrial complex, the environment, and the rise of the Far Right.

INSTITUTE FOR ANARCHIST STUDIES GRANTS UPDATE

THE INSTITUTE FOR ANARCHIST STUDIES (IAS) IS REFORMULATING OUR grants program. Beginning in 2019, we will implement a new approach to funding antiauthoritarian work.

For the first 22 years of our existence, the IAS has awarded money to applications involving the written word, from original essays to translations and scripts. We would like to expand that now to include other media, such as podcasts and videos, with the goal of increasing our outreach and accessibility. At the end of each summer, we will select a current and relevant theme based on ongoing work and questions facing our movement. Successful grant applications will be geared toward this topic or inquiry, and our publications, journal, and multimedia for the year will engage a range of intersecting perspectives.

Each year, we will set out to raise money for basic operating costs and, beyond that, to award grants in support of projects addressing the annual theme. The amount that we are able to offer will be based upon the success of our fundraising. If we are not able to award significant, need-based funding in a given year, we plan to offer smaller, equally-distributed amounts to our writers, as we believe in supporting both the material and intellectual needs of our contributors.

We are very excited about this expansion of our work. Stay tuned later this fall for announcements about the themes we're looking for and how to apply for funding. Meanwhile, please become a monthly sustainer to make this work possible!

Go to PayPal and pledge a monthly donation via our email address: anarchiststudies@gmail.com.

SUPPORT THE IAS

The Institute for Anarchist Studies relies on financial support from you to do its work. We are a largely volunteer-run organization—proof that a small number of dedicated individuals can produce inspiring results! We aim to further anarchist analysis and to spread the influence of antiauthoritarian ideas and praxis through reflection, dialogue, and education. Our work takes many forms, including:

★ Grants for radical writers & translators
★ *Perspectives on Anarchist Theory* journal (both online and in print)
★ Anarchist Interventions and other book series through AK Press
★ The Mutual Aid Speakers Bureau
★ Sponsorship of educational events
★ And more!

By including the Institute for Anarchist Studies in your will, you can memorialize your commitment to liberatory struggles and ensure that our shared vision of a free society carries on.

A bequest to the IAS is easy to arrange and can be made by including the following words in your will:

"I give to Institute for Anarchist Studies (**Federal Tax ID #81-3419050**), a 501©(3) nonprofit organization with its principal mailing address at PO Box 90454, Portland, OR 97290, ___% of my estate [or: the sum of $___] to be used in such a manner as the Board of Directors of the Institute for Anarchist Studies shall, in its sole discretion, determine."

Any type of cash, securities, personal property, or real estate can be given through a bequest. The IAS can also be named beneficiary of assets that often pass outside a will, such as IRAs, pension plans, life insurance, or assets held in a trust or annuity. To do so, contact the relevant institution and complete the appropriate beneficiary designation form.

For more information about the Institute for Anarchist Studies, and to discuss your gift, please contact us at anarchiststudies@gmail.com.